Greek Sanctuaries

Greek
Sanctuaries

R. A. TOMLINSON

Book Club Associates
London

This edition published 1976 by
Book Club Associates
by arrangement with Paul Elek Ltd. London

Printed in Great Britain by litho by The Anchor Press Ltd
and bound by Wm Brendon & Son Ltd
both of Tiptree, Essex

Contents

Plates

Between pages 80 and 81

Figures

The drawings are by Harry Buglass of the Department of Ancient History and Archaeology at the University of Birmingham.

Acknowledgements

I am greatly indebted to the British School of Archaeology at Athens; this book was completed, and most of the photographs made when I held the Visiting Fellowship there in 1975. The debt, however, is of much longer standing. I am grateful to friends and colleagues in Greece elsewhere; particularly to Stephen Miller, who showed me his excavations at Nemea. I must also express my gratitude to the Directors of the German Institute and the French School at Athens for permission to use as the base of plans in this book their plans of Olympia, Delphi, Delos, and Epidauros; and to W. B. Dinsmoor, Jnr, for his permission to use drawings of the temples of Poseidon at Isthmia which appeared in Volume I of *Isthmia*.

Preface

The number of religious sanctuaries which once existed among the ancient Greek city-states cannot be calculated. We know about them from a variety of sources—from archaeological evidence, from the ancient authors, from records inscribed on stone—but none of these is at all complete. Sanctuaries previously unknown are still reported by the archaeologist, the literary evidence is limited in extent and preservation, the record on inscriptions variable. In this book an attempt is made to give a general introduction to the architecture and arrangement of sanctuaries, as well as the more formal side of their organization. More detailed accounts of various sanctuaries are intended as a sample, or cross-section, ranging from the most important to those of purely local significance. Even so, the choice depends on information being available; and of the simplest sanctuaries, often completely unmonumental in character, there is little which can be said. It should not be thought that the small cross-section is entirely representative, and there are certain areas, particularly the Greek colonies of the West and in North Africa, which I have totally omitted, being largely extensions of the Doric tradition of the mainland.

Greek place names and other Greek words generally have been transliterated to the equivalent letters of our alphabet—thus k when the Greek word used *kappa*, rather than the Latinized c. Latinized forms are used where they are the more familiar (thus Boeotia, not Boiotia) and English forms where they are established (thus Athens, not Athenai).

I   Introduction – the Bronze Age

The origins of Greek religion, not surprisingly, are as obscure and confused as those of the Greeks themselves. By the time the sanctuaries to be described in this book had arrived at a definitive form, various peoples at widely differing periods of time had made their way into the Greek peninsular. The last significant movement had come at about the beginning of the first millennium BC, when people speaking the Dorian and other related dialects of the Greek language had migrated into southern Greece, probably from the mountainous areas in the north-west of the peninsular where previously they had been somewhat (though not completely) cut off from the forms of civilization developed in the Aegean areas.[1] In the Aegean area Greeks speaking other dialects (the ancestors of dialects which were spoken in the classical period) had been established probably since the beginning of the second millennium, and were responsible for the creation of substantial communities, centred on an elaborate palace administrative centre, such as Mycenae and Tiryns in the Argolid, and Pylos in Messenia, the south-western part of the mainland.[2] These were sophisticated places, in contact with the non-Greek civilization of Crete (where the Greeks eventually took control) and the Near East, the Levant and Egypt. Though these Greeks may well have brought with them religious concepts similar to those of the remoter Dorians, they were obviously subject to the influences of the non-Greek communities with which they were in contact; of these, Crete is likely to have been particularly influential.

In the remoter prehistoric period there may well have been movements, difficult enough to trace from the purely material remains they have left behind and impossible to assess in terms of religion. The influence of trading partners, on whom the Greeks depended for their prosperity, is also of importance, though the exact weight which should be attributed to this factor is uncertain; the Greeks themselves traced much of their religion to eastern originals, to Egypt and to the Phoenician communities of the Levant. Herodotus[3] points out similarities between them (though he is also aware of considerable differences) and since he, and other Greeks, knew that these other civilizations were much older than that of the Greeks, he naturally assigned to them the derivation of the Greek cults. Near Eastern trade had been resumed on a substantial scale in the eighth century BC; direct contact with Egypt came a little later.[4] By the Hellenistic age, the late fourth and third centuries BC, cults from these areas were definitely established in Greece in recognizable form.

It is not the purpose of this book to elucidate the differing influences discernible in the religion of Greece during the classical period. It is, rather, an attempt to describe the sanctuaries as they then were, and to explain the way in which they functioned. Greek religion was not exclusive. The Greeks in their primitive origins, which in reality were not far removed from the apparent sophistication of the classical age, were in awe of the universal power exerted on the fortunes of mankind by the supernatural. When they moved to a new region, they dared not supplant local religious ideas, for fear that some god might be offended. Equally, the deliberate introduction of a new cult might confer benefits, in winning the favour of a god whose existence, through ignorance, had been neglected. The following account of the main forms of Greek religion and its related architecture necessarily omits much of the variation which is one of its chief fascinations.

It is not unlikely that the first essential formative period, in which primitive ideas began to evolve towards the religious concepts of the classical era was the late Bronze Age. The classical civilization of the first millennium BC was not the first in Greece. Highly organized states, attaining considerable wealth, existed there already in the second part of the preceding millennium, deriving much from the neighbouring island of Crete, but emerging, by the fourteenth century BC, to a dominant position in the mainland and the area of the Aegean Sea. This, the civilization of the late Bronze Age, disintegrated in the twelfth century, when Greece began to relapse into an isolated and more primitive state, but at least a memory of the former glories remained in the epic poems which told of Agamemnon, King of Mycenae and over-lord of all Greece, who led the Greeks to Troy, and after a ten-year siege, destroyed that city. Some of the monuments of this bygone age, its tombs and its fortifications, were visible and known in classical Greece, but it has been left to the modern archaeo-logist to discover its essential achievements in Greece, and those of Cretan civilization which preceded it, as well as Troy, which it destroyed.

The epic poems were composed, orally, after the event, handed down and modified by succeeding generations. The classical Greeks attributed the greatest of them, the *Iliad* and the *Odyssey*, to Homer, the blind poet who, the best authorities believed, lived in the eighth century BC, long after the events his poems described, compiling them from the traditional stories which had been transmitted by word of mouth. Even Homer did not write them down, and it is unlikely that they achieved written form until the sixth century BC. As a result, it is impossible to be certain that anything they contain refers essentially to the late Bronze Age, and was not added later. Even so, the gods play such an important role in the unfolding of the stories that it is totally impossible for them to be merely a later accretion. Thus the poems can be considered to shed some light on the forms and nature of Greek religion before the classical period.

In Homer the gods are readily identifiable with those of the classical age. They have the same names and the same functions. Zeus is the father of the gods, Poseidon is lord of the sea, Apollo sends the plague, and so on. They are anthropomorphic in form and nature. They have the same appetites and desires as men. Their society is essentially an eternal version of the heroic society of the kings and princes whose deeds dominate the poems. In the Trojan war they take sides. The quarrel was caused by the rivalry between the goddesses Hera, Athena and Aphrodite, and the judgement of Paris, son of Priam, the Trojan king, who gave the prize for beauty, not sur-prisingly, to Aphrodite, the goddess of love. Zeus, the husband of Hera and father of Athena, is the arbiter; Hera favours the Trojans, Athena the Greeks, and the fortunes of war incline from side to side as the impartial Zeus listens now to one goddess, now to the other. In such episodes one gains the impression that the whole destiny of man is controlled by the gods, who manipulate him like a puppet, though, because of their uncertainty, his fate is not predetermined. It is possible, therefore, for a man to take action to win the support and favour of the gods. This is done, largely, by offerings to them; if the gods are pleased, they look favourably on the men who make the offering. Similarly, their anger may be turned aside by a suitably imposing sacrifice. The gods appear among men and talk directly to them (or, at least, to the more important heroes), but when they do this they usually take the guise of a recognizable human: it is only when the conversation is finished that the hero realizes he has been talking to a god. The gods have shrines and images, which form a focus of ritual, but the offerings are made at an altar; the sacrifice and burning at the altar of cattle or other animals is the usual form, the god being attracted and pleased by the smell as the smoke wafts its way up to the skies. The gods have under their protection particular regions of Greece, but their dwelling place is on Mount Olympus in northern Greece, between the districts of Thessaly and Macedon. There is also the underworld, where the shadows of the dead reside, like insubstantial ghosts. These are placated by other means. Being dead they lack blood; they can thus be revived by offerings of blood, poured direct from the victim into a pit.

The archaeological evidence relating to religion in Greece during the Bronze Age is far from clear.[5] Recently what appears to have been a centre of cult has been discovered on the citadel of Mycenae, among the subordinate buildings of the lower slopes rather than the main administrative centre, the palace, on the top of the hill.[6] It consisted of a set of rooms, of irregular plan and arrangement. On a platform were painted horns of consecration (a regular Cretan religious symbol). Sealed up in a small storeroom (perhaps to conceal them at a time of imminent attack, rather than for any religious reason) were a number of terracotta figures, mostly female, and two complete terracotta coiled snakes (together with fragments of at least eleven others). Similar terracotta figures have been found in excavations of a Late Bronze Age shrine building on the island of Keos.[7] Access to this storeroom from the main room (which was at a lower level) was by way of a stone staircase. A platform adjoined this; on it was found another female figure, with a clay offering table; there were other platforms by the wall of this room which was of substantial size. In an adjacent part (apparently without inter-communication) was a large room, its walls decorated with frescoes of female figures and of a male in female dress. A platform at right angles to the fresco bore painted horns of consecration.

Despite this evidence for Cretan influence, the religion of the mainland in the Bronze Age required other, non-Cretan arrangements. Cult buildings as such were not used (the Cretan-inspired terracottas in the shrines at Mycenae and Keos prove the abnormality of these structures), and it is usually supposed that cult practices centred in the principal room of the palace, emphasizing the role of the king in religion.[8] In the porch of the principal room at Mycenae remains of an altar for burnt offerings and offering tables were found. At Pylos there was an object identified as a portable altar by the great central hearth of the principal room, and a fixed altar in a courtyard in the north-east wing of the palace. The palace at Tiryns also had an altar, a circular one this time, in the courtyard, in line with the door of the principal room. Thus there seems to have been provision in the Bronze Age palaces of the mainland for burnt offerings at open-air altars, from which the smoke would be able to ascend to the gods in the sky.

The roles of the portable altars and the great hearths of the principal rooms of the

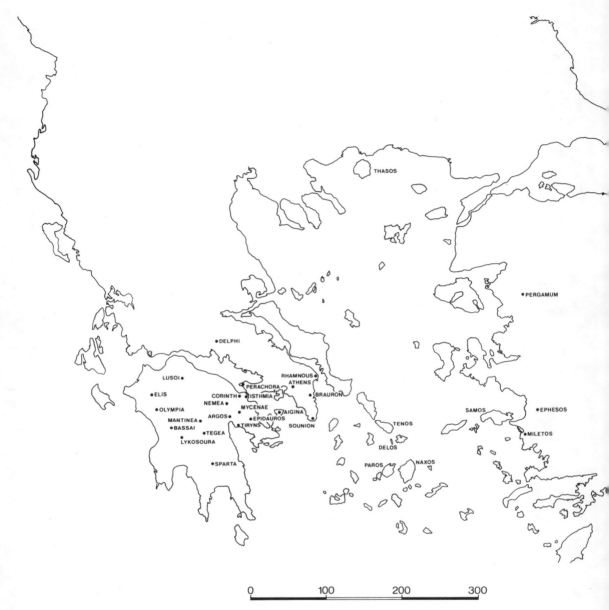

1 Map of Greece

palaces are less certain. Some 'portable altars' are more likely to have functioned as braziers to warm the rooms in the occasionally unpleasant cold of winter; such a function might suggest that they are purely utilitarian. Their presence in tombs may be explained by the feeling that the dead required the equipment of real life; but the possibility of a religious function, as an altar, is now stronger. When they are found by the hearth of the principal room, which would have given sufficient heat, a

14

religious function seems assured. Portable altars are, in fact, known and used in later classical religion. Whether the hearth itself was primarily or significantly a place of cult might be doubted. That libations were poured at the hearth and personal offerings made at banquets and other gatherings seems reasonable; but the concept of the hearth as the focus of essentially religious activity seems derived from the belief that it fulfilled this role in later Greek religion, and the fact that 'hearth altars' have been identified in later temple buildings. This later identification is open to serious doubt,[9] and it seems safer not to extend this concept back into the Bronze Age. Conversely, it is dangerous to use this interpretation of the role played by the hearth in Bronze Age religion as the origin of later practice.

There is a long gap between the destruction of the Bronze Age palaces, and the re-emergence of the developed civilization in Greece which created the sanctuaries (fig. 1). Yet it is not possible that Greece during this period was totally depopulated, and some forms of religious belief and practice must have lingered in the old areas, to be joined by the cults of the newcomers who migrated to them.[10] Such, however, is the essential poverty of this dark age that the material evidence for the practice of religion does not survive. Even so, there seems no reason to doubt the fundamental importance of these earlier ages to the development of classical Greek religion and its sanctuaries.

2   The sanctuaries of the classical age

When, in the eighteenth century AD, interest in the antiquities of classical Greece revived, it was the temples which attracted the attention of architects.[1] The solemn, simple forms of the Doric order, the more delicate elaboration of the Ionic were lauded in preference to the ornate Roman forms.[2] The Greek temples were measured, drawn, studied and even copied by the architects of Europe, and the neo-classical style was born.[3] As a result, the originals are more often admired for their architectural qualities than interpreted in terms of their function. The greatest temples, it is true, were intended to impress mortals almost as much as the gods to whom they were dedicated; but the essential function of the temple was religious, and they are best appreciated not as isolated museum pieces but as integral elements in the practice of ancient Greek religion.

Classical Greek religion, like that of the Homeric poems, was anthropomorphic. It recognized a variety of supernatural powers, which controlled, each with its own special concern, the different elements of life and nature. These gods had the appearance of human beings, male and female; with greater than human power, it is true, and endowed with the blessing of immortality, but their needs and passions were akin to those of ordinary men. If they were pleased—or placated—they would confer benefits and protection on their human subjects. They had to be housed, and given, as befitted their status, the best house in the community; they required food, and they responded favourably to the offering of valuable gifts.

The gods were thus part of the community in which they existed—and in many senses, the ruling element in the community, for the affairs of the Greeks were strictly controlled by the laws of their religion; even at the height of internecine war the religious truce which permitted the celebration of the Olympic religious festival (of which the games were part) had to be observed. The power of the gods extended over all the Greek world, and could ignore the human boundaries of the city-states. At the same time they were concerned, individually, with the fortunes of the separate cities, and each city had one special god or goddess whose particular concern was its protection—and for whom, of course, the most spectacular temple was built. Thus the gods of the Greeks were at the same time local and universal. The principal gods had their abode on Mount Olympus, in northern Greece, remote from the main centres of the classical world; but they also had their homes in the individual cities. Religion, and therefore architectural interest, centred on these local residences, and there were no temples on the summit of Mount Olympus, for their home there was built by the gods themselves.

Though the temple was the building in which the god was supposed to live, and which in fact housed a statue or less lifelike image representing him, it was not the focal point of the religious ritual performed in his honour. This took place at an altar, at which offerings (usually of food and normally of meat) were made to him in the presence of a gathering of human worshippers. These rituals were held regularly, but infrequently, normally at annual intervals. The procedure was in the form of a religious festival, of which the offering at the altar was only a part; other aspects might include processions, dances, dramatic performances and athletic contests. Offerings other than food might be required. At the Great Panathenaic festival held at Athens to worship the protecting (and eponymous) goddess Athena, the standard principal offerings included a cow, which was sacrificed and eaten, and a suit of bronze armour, which was then kept in a special building on the Acropolis called the Armoury (*Chalkotheke*).[4] In addition, the maidens of Athens wove a new robe, the *peplos*, which clothed the venerable wooden cult-statue of the goddess.[5] Thus the temples should never be considered in isolation. They should be studied rather in relation to the total complex of buildings and monuments with which they were associated, the religious sanctuaries of the Greek world.

A sanctuary was an area set aside for the uses of religion, and the cult of a particular god, or, perhaps, an associated group of gods. It had no fixed form or size, and the particular places selected as suitable localities for sanctuaries varied considerably in character. All these things depended on the importance of the cult, and the community which established it. Some sanctuaries served the most powerful of the cities, and were the scene of festivals which attracted worshippers in tens of thousands; some, such as Delphi or Delos, though situated in states which were themselves of minor rank, had a religious importance which extended over a wide area of the Greek world; others served the local needs of small communities, or sections of communities. This wide range of importance is naturally reflected in the wide variations of size and magnificence which the sanctuaries show. Certain features are, of course, essential, but even here the precise form varied. A sanctuary had to be set apart from the secular world which surrounded it, and therefore required a precise boundary. This might be marked by a wall, and entered through a formal gateway or *propylon*; or it could be defined simply by a series of marker stones, entry to the sanctuary being merely a matter of crossing an imaginary line between two of them. Religiously, both systems had the same function; architecturally, in terms of visual appearance, the differences are of course considerable. The *shape* of the sanctuary depends on the area of land available for it, and is normally irregular; but where it occurs in a planned city (of which there are numerous examples in the Greek world) with streets arranged in a grid plan, then the sanctuary may be strictly rectangular. This form lends itself to symmetrical and axial planning within the sanctuary itself; otherwise the siting of buildings in the sanctuary, though often visually harmonious, is rarely rigidly planned.

Within the sanctuary, the chief requirement was not the temple but rather the altar. Here was the fire at which the burnt offerings were made and it was here that the central act of sacrifice was performed, watched by the worshippers. Since the smell of the burnt offering was supposed to drift up through the air to the gods, the altar was normally in the open; the worshippers stood around it, also in the open. Again, there is a wide variety both of form and size. The altars were usually of stone (though that of Zeus at Olympia was simply the pile of ashes from former sacrifices). It might consist of a single block, with little carved decoration, or a major structure of considerable architectural complexity, such as the Great Altar of Pergamon. It was usually situated in front of the temple, if there was one; that is, to the east of it, giving the cult-image in the temple a view of the sacrifice. The sacrificing priest would stand at the altar, again normally facing east. Nevertheless, these rules were not inflexible, and though the positioning of the altar in front of the temple on a strict axial alignment is very common, there are numerous examples where there is no such formal relationship.

There is a similar wide variety in the forms of the temples. The temple essentially housed the cult-statue, and might therefore be merely a simple shrine-like building. The varying degrees of elaboration depended on several factors. The temple itself was an offering to the god; the more important the cult to the community in which it was situated, or to the people who came to it from outside, the more splendid the temple would be. It reflected also the material wealth and prestige of the community, and though even a poor community would normally devote a disproportionate amount of its material resources to the construction of its principal temple, the resulting building would inevitably be less splendid than the temples of rich and powerful communities such as Athens. Here again it is the latter which are of architectural interest; but the former, and the sanctuaries in which they stood, are no less important in the history of Greek religion.

Other buildings, structures and monuments are found in Greek sanctuaries, though it is not possible to generalize about them in the same way. Again, much of their interest lies in the bewildering variety. Here, in particular, are the differences between one sanctuary and another, and they can only be described satisfactorily in the individual accounts of the sanctuaries in which they are found. It is possible to categorize the different buildings, but it must be remembered that none is essential, nor does every sanctuary contain examples of all of them. Sanctuaries were intended to house offerings made to the gods. Where these were durable—statues, for example— they might stand simply in the open air, in the sanctuary. Others were more delicate, or valuable, and needed to be protected, possibly under lock and key for the sanctity which invariably attached to such gifts could not always guarantee their security. They were often housed in the temple itself, at the sides of its inner room, on galleries constructed to receive them, or even under the roof on a floor laid above the ceiling beams. Often there was not enough room in the temples for such offerings. Therefore an important category of additional building comprises shelters and storerooms—the Armoury on the Acropolis of Athens is an example. The more important of them usually have colonnaded porches or façades; frequently these take the form of extensive porticoes, with or without rooms behind, which the Greeks called *stoas*. At first these, like the temples, were free-standing buildings, often situated to one side of the sanctuary, from which people could watch the activities round the temple and altar. Later they gained in architectural importance, and in their most elaborate form are incorporated with the boundary wall of the sanctuary, completely surrounding the sanctuary with inward facing colonnades, framing the temple and the other monuments within it. This type was particularly favoured for the strictly rectangular sanctuaries in planned cities. Many sanctuaries contain buildings which are often described as 'priests' houses', and which seem to reflect some of the characteristics shown by residential buildings. Such an interpretation is often based on dubious inference. Sometimes the written accounts which have survived from antiquity refer to priests or priestesses living in the sanctuary, and provision must have been made for their accommodation. We shall see examples of buildings with rooms specially equipped for dining in the Greek manner, either in or immediately adjacent to the sanctuary. These are often interpreted as priests' houses, or at least rooms in which the priests dined; but the identification of the group that used them is an assumption—they may, for example, have been used by the political rather than the religious leaders of the community—and unless there is written evidence for the use of a building by priests, these structures are best not described as priests' houses. It must be remembered that ancient Greek religion did not normally employ a full-time clergy, comparable with that of the Christian church, but assigned priestly duties to prominent citizens, who would also follow a secular career. Certain cults did have permanent full-time priests or, frequently, priestesses. From an inscription we hear of the appointment at Athens of a priestess of Nike (Victory), the salary she was paid and the other perquisites—the skins of the sacrificial animals, which presumably, could be sold; but there is no evidence that she lived on the Acropolis.[6]

In some sanctuaries it is possible to distinguish between the area of strict sanctity and an adjacent, ancillary area.[7] The former included, obviously, the temple and the altar, but other buildings were not necessarily excluded, particularly if there were a large number of offerings which required housing. In addition, this part might contain dedicatory monuments, whether given by the state or private individuals. The outer area, where it can be recognized, would be concerned more with human activities, the games, the dramatic and choral performances, the feasting. If the areas can be separated, there is likely to be a formal propylon serving as the entrance to the area of strict sanctity. An excellent example of this arrangement has been identified at the sanctuary of Herakles on the island of Thasos;[8] here the inner area included originally an altar and nothing else. To this was added, first, a formal dining-room (later increased to a set of five rooms side by side, with a stoa in front), then a peripteral temple (that is, a temple surrounded by a colonnade), and an elongated room with several doors, perhaps to house offerings but of uncertain purpose, the whole area being then marked off and entered through a formal gateway on the west side. This gateway, however, was only a formal entrance, since it was flanked on both sides by a series of steps leading up to the area in front of the altar. It is more likely that these were not used for access (which would have been prevented by a taboo, rather than a physical barrier) but as a place from which spectators could watch contests taking place in the secondary area outside the sanctuary. It was in this secondary area that in Hellenistic times a large square building with a substantial columnar porch and an inner colonnaded court was built, probably to provide more elaborate dining accommodation.

The same distinction might be noted in Christian sanctuaries of present-day Greece, particularly in the rural areas. Here, on the feast day of the saint to whom the church is dedicated, a festival is held. Inside the church the worshippers watch the enactment of the sacred liturgy by the priest in the holy of holies and in front of the ikon screen; this corresponds to the temple, the altar, and the open space round the altar. Outside, in the churchyard, which is marked off from the secular world by a wall but is not an area as strictly sacred as the church, more mundane activities involving, say, swings for the children and roasting of meat are celebrated in terms of purely human enjoyment. The derivation of this from ancient practice is clear.

Greek religion had a strong contractual element in it. The favour of the gods was obtained by gifts, made either voluntarily, in anticipation of benefits, or in payment promised should the benefit be conferred. The offering might be small and comparatively valueless—a simple terracotta vase, for example. It might be of great intrinsic value—gold cups and bowls. It might be substantial—a statue or group of statues or a stone seat. All, in their different ways, affected the appearance of the sanctuaries. The more precious objects had to be kept under lock and key, whether in the temples or the special storerooms built to house them. The humble offerings were placed in a suitable location, on and around the temples. The more substantial monuments stood in the sanctuary, which was thus not a simple arrangement of major buildings and the altar; the size, number, form and positioning of these offerings must have affected the appearance of the sanctuary profoundly. Here again no fixed rules appear, and no two sanctuaries are alike. In some the placing of monuments appears quite haphazard, in others more regular. Since there were often defined lines of communication within the sanctuaries, particularly the larger ones, routes along which processions passed, and so forth, and since one of the reasons for setting up a monument was, in a sense, self-advertisement (for inscriptions on the monument usually proclaimed who the donor was), the sides of these routes were often a favoured place for the positioning of monuments (plate 1).

Just as the forms of the sanctuaries vary, so also do their histories. The Greeks often traced the origins of the sanctuaries back to the remote pre-classical past, to the years which we would describe as belonging to the Bronze Age of the second millennium BC. We have seen that there is strong evidence to suggest that classical Greek religion owes much to its Bronze Age antecedents; that, at the least, the gods were the same and had the same names. It is also likely that in some (but not all) regions and cities the principal gods of the classical age were those who had been important in the Bronze Age. The archaeological evidence for continuity is less certain. This evidence is primarily in the form of objects, or fragments of objects, deposited in the area of the sanctuary, and the buildings with which these objects are archaeologically associated. From the eighth century BC onwards some of these, particularly the pottery, which survives in considerable quantities, may be recognized as having a specifically religious nature or purpose; for example, miniature vases, too small to have any practical use, were made specially to be offered to the gods, as tokens, as it were. Often, the identification of a religious purpose in any object is subjective, and, therefore, proves nothing. Few—very few—sanctuaries show continuity in the depositing of objects from the Bronze Age to the succeeding millennium. Even where objects of the Bronze Age are found, it is often difficult to demonstrate an essentially religious function for them, while, with the latest Bronze Age objects belonging to the twelfth century BC, and the earliest of the succeeding millennium to the eighth, it is impossible to provide the archaeological bridge necessary to prove continuity. The information provided by the architectural evidence is similar, for nowhere can a continuous sequence of buildings be proved to have existed. Yet the probability of continuity in some form remains an atttractive hypothesis. A comparison between the architectural arrangement of a Bronze Age 'palace', such as that at Tiryns, and a classical sanctuary, such as that of Athena on the Acropolis at Athens, shows such striking similarity that it is hard to believe that it results simply from coincidence. Both are entered through a propylon, whose walls form a letter H in plan, with the entrance doors (one at

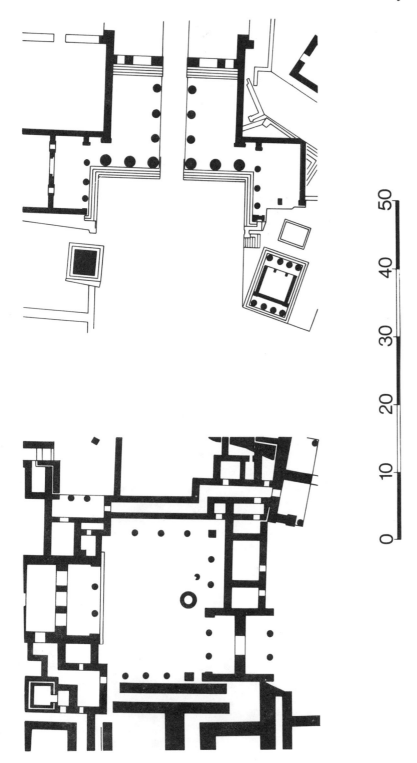

2 Gateway to the Bronze Age palace, Tiryns (left) compared with the classical propylaia, Athens

Tiryns, more than one at Athens—fig. 2) in the cross-stroke and columns in front and behind. This leads to a courtyard, which could have accommodated a crowd of people; at the back is the main building whose essential plan is similar, both in the palace and the classical sanctuary. It must be remembered that in the Bronze Age the Acropolis at Athens, with its stronghold walls comparable with those of the palace of Tiryns, was the site for a similar palace; but even so, it hardly seems possible that the Bronze Age buildings survived long enough to be the examples for classical successors. The possibility of continuity nevertheless remains.

Otherwise, it appears that many sanctuaries first developed beyond the non-monumental concept of the place of sacrifice in the eighth century BC; a few may be earlier, many, of course, are much later. The eighth century was, in general, an age of revival and development in the Greek world, marking the real end of the dark age which had followed the collapse of Bronze Age civilization. If there was no real continuity from the Bronze Age, the alternative hypothesis is attractive—that the Greeks began to develop religious sanctuaries in imitation of those that they had seen overseas (particularly in the Levant) as a result of the renewal of overseas trading contacts in that century. Here again, archaeological proof is uncertain. Sanctuaries, of course, existed in the Levant communities but are not simply copied by the Greeks. It seems best to argue that the development of sanctuaries at this time in Greece is a direct result of the growth in material prosperity, in which the gods, as an essential part of the community, were bound to have their share.

During the seventh and sixth centuries the sanctuaries developed and flourished. Most show successive improvements in their buildings as architectural techniques, methods and the materials employed improve, partly as a result of the inventiveness of the Greeks, partly through the extension of their experience of other peoples and traditions. The temples become larger and rather more elaborate externally; with the development of stone construction they approach their definitive form. In addition, the sanctuaries received an abundance of offerings, metalwork in gold, silver and bronze, some of which has fortunately survived, and quantities of the fine painted pottery which is one of the greatest achievements of Greek craft during these centuries, in particular the delicate wares from Corinth. By the end of the sixth century almost all the important sanctuaries of the Greek world were well established and patronized. Many had buildings which continued in use to the end of the classical cults, and even survived, abandoned or converted to other purposes, beyond that time. Though there was still much building to be done, and many more monuments to be dedicated to the use of the gods, the forms were definitively established.

At the end of the sixth and beginning of the fifth centuries came the disruption caused by the rise of the Persian Empire, the conquest of the east Greek cities and the invasions of mainland Greece by Darius and Xerxes (together with the contemporary attack on the west Greek cities of Sicily by the Carthaginians). Much damage was done, and much rebuilding was necessary. Even in sanctuaries untouched by the invaders the triumph of Greece over the barbarians led to the construction of new temples, and new trophies were set up commemorating the victories. Damaged buildings and particularly the smaller monuments were demolished, but since they were still the property of the gods they could not properly be removed from the sanctuaries by mere men; so they were buried and concealed from sight, to be rediscovered by archaeologists in the nineteenth and twentieth centuries, and so to give us a much clearer insight into the earlier history of the sanctuaries than we might otherwise possess.

By the fifth century there are signs of a decline in the economic condition of the Greek world. This is concealed, to a certain extent, by the emergence of Athens as the leader of the Aegean Greeks against the continued threat of Persia. This leadership enabled her to control the wealth of the cities subject to her, and to extract from them payment of tribute. She was thus given the resources of a considerable architectural programme, the building of temples in the major sanctuaries of the city and elsewhere. In many ways these buildings represent the height of Greek architectural achievement, and they have assumed, quite naturally, a dominating position in our understanding of Greek temples. The other monuments in the sanctuaries, the ancillary buildings, and, above all, the sculpture also reached a definitive form and degree of splendour which set the pattern for the remainder of the classical age. The archaeological evidence for offerings is more scanty, though this may give a distorted picture. Corinthian pottery was no longer made,[9] and though Athenian pottery had, largely, replaced it, it is not found in such quantities in the sanctuaries. There is more evidence in the form of temple inventories, recorded on stone, of the contents of the sanctuaries, which show that valuable objects were there in abundance, and the lists added to regularly.[10] Perhaps the true impression is that the offerings in general were more valuable than in previous centuries, and that relatively humble gifts such as pottery were less frequent.

It is not until the succeeding fourth century that, following the self-destructive war between Athens and Sparta, the economic difficulties of the Greek world noticeably affected the development of the sanctuaries. Athenian building was at a standstill from 406 to the 340s; and though this period sees the beginning of the great construction programme in the Epidaurian sanctuary of Asklepios, it is not until the final part of the fourth century that it reaches substantial achievement; some of the buildings seem to have taken an inordinately long time to complete. Signs of poverty and disruption are clear; piracy was rampant in the Aegean, while the west Greek communities gradually lost their independence to the resurgent Italians, dominated increasingly by Rome. Even worse than the decline of offerings made in the sanctuaries was the growing habit of plundering them of the valuables they contained to finance the mercenary armies used in what appears almost as an incessant pattern of warfare towards the middle of the century. The greatest sanctuaries with their enormous wealth were particularly subject to this. Olympia was plundered by Arcadian cities in 364 (though restitution was subsequently made for this) and Delphi by the Phocians in 353. A low point in the fortunes of the Greeks, and therefore of their sanctuaries also, was reached at the middle of the century.

The subsequent revival was due to Persian gold, paid first, probably, as a subsidy by the Persian kings in an attempt to avert the threat of invasion. Then, after the invasion successfully led by Alexander the Great had brought about the complete conquest of the Persian Empire, gold captured by his army was released from the treasure houses of the defeated Persians. The revival came too late to save the western Greeks, though Syracuse flourished into the third century BC. In mainland Greece the impetus seems to die away in the third century, though certain sanctuaries flourished, and some, the recipients still of subsidies from one or other of the Hellenistic kings who took over the control of Alexander's divided empire, continued to construct new buildings and substantial monuments until Greece was incorporated into the Roman Empire. Otherwise, depopulation and a redistribution of wealth led, apparently, to the abandonment or virtual neglect of the less important sanctuaries in particular. In the east Greek area, freed from Persian rule and flourishing economically, the picture of prosperity and development lasts much longer.

These trends are confirmed in Roman times. The sanctuaries of mainland Greece seem to have continued fitfully, but their buildings and other monuments are complete. Occasionally the particular interest of a Roman ruler—Julius Caesar, Nero or Hadrian—or an individual multi-millionaire such as Herodes Atticus in the second century AD would bring about a flurry of building activity in places which commanded their special favour. At Thasos, for example, the outer part of the sanctuary of Herakles, opposite the Hellenistic dining-court, was given an elaborate entrance in the form of a Roman triumphal arch by the emperor Caracalla, as late as the first part of the third century AD. But the old cults, essentially involved in the Greek rather than the Roman political system, could no longer command universal respect or devotion, and the sanctuaries inevitably suffered. Even worse were the active depredations of other Roman leaders who removed statues—even when they were integral parts of the temples—to adorn Rome. Certain sanctuaries, those of the mystery cults more concerned with the salvation of the individual than the state, flourished, but these were few. The great majority of the sanctuaries seem to have been dead long before the conversion of the Empire to Christianity brought about their official closure.[11] In the more prosperous cities of the east Greek area development was continued into the Roman period, and new temples and other structures of architectural importance and merit were built. Yet even here, the classical religions had to succumb, and by the mid-fourth century AD the sanctuaries were closed.

Thus it is with the early, archaic period, from the eighth to the sixth century, and the classical age of the fifth and less importantly the fourth century BC that we are concerned, with some extension into later ages. The first is an age of pioneering development, the second of the refinement of established form to approach perfection as close as was humanly possible; thereafter, it is a matter of the continuance or revival of a tradition.

Needless to say, no Greek sanctuary has come down to us intact. The degree of devastation varies. The causes of this are equally varied. If the buildings are converted to other purposes, and continue to be used, the chances of survival are quite good, given the superbly solid construction of the more important structures. Temples were on occasion converted to Christian churches. The conversion usually follows after a period of disuse, rather than a sudden alteration of religious occupation, and requires some modification of the structure since temples were not designed to hold congregations. A good example is the temple of Athena at Syracuse, where the spaces between the outer columns have been filled to form a wall, and the former wall within the colonnade opened up to create the aisle and nave form of a Christian church. Two temples in Athens owe their good, or relatively good, state of preservation to continued religious use, the temple of Hephaistos as a church, the Parthenon as a church and then, after the Turkish conquest, a mosque. The continued use need not be religious; some buildings are incorporated into fortifications, others converted into houses (the Turkish Governor of Athens kept his harem in the Erechtheion).

When buildings are totally abandoned, their eventual destruction is virtually assured, unless they are in regions so remote and unfrequented that the human agency necessary for their dismantling is absent; then they suffer only from natural causes of collapse. Much of the Greek world is liable to earthquake, and though the more important buildings were constructed to be, as far as possible, resistant to earthquake, nothing the Greeks could design was capable of withstanding the occasional major tremors. Often the position of the ruins shows the evidence of earthquake destruction, columns laid out in rows, walls laid flat, but with their blocks still in their correct relationship to each other. The inevitable forces of decay have also caused widespread destruction. Most Greek buildings had roofs supported on timber beams. Once these had decayed the roofs collapsed. Stone walls were damaged in consequence, walls of unbaked brick (very frequent in the minor buildings of sanctuaries) were dissolved in the rain. Nevertheless, human action was the most destructive. This might have had various motives. The neat, substantial squared blocks of Greek masonry had obvious uses as building material, and were often removed to serve other purposes (columns, being less obviously useful, were more likely to survive).[12] Marble and limestone were frequently burned in kilns to provide lime and here whole buildings might have been consumed. There were less immediately obvious reasons for deliberate destruction. One of the methods the Greeks used to protect their major buildings from the effects of earthquake was to clamp the blocks together, with iron clamps set in lead. Though the amount of metal used was small, in later times it was valuable, and buildings were often torn apart to recover it. Less logical, but still a potent force for destruction, was the Greek peasants' belief that anything ancient contains gold, and it is not unlikely that buildings were broken up in a vain quest for it.

The other monuments, the gifts and offerings, suffered equally varied fates. Those of valuable metal were obviously at great risk; but they occasionally survive if they were buried while the sanctuary was still functioning, or were otherwise lost to sight before any deliberate act of plunder. Objects of bronze had a higher chance of survival, but again might be removed, once the sanctuary was abandoned, for the intrinsic value of their metal. Bronze statues were particularly vulnerable, and many sanctuaries still contain statue bases of stone bearing the imprint where bronze statues were once fixed to them; occasionally, in the thieves' haste to remove the bulk of the metal, the statue has been broken off at the ankles, leaving the feet still fixed to the base. The stone monuments—bases, columns, seats—were more likely to survive, and stone statues might have escaped the lime-kiln or the Roman collector; but it is the valueless (except to the archaeologist) broken fragments of pottery which survive in the greatest quantities, creating (as we have seen) a possibly misleading picture of the prosperity of a sanctuary, for it seems likely that pottery was not given in such quantities in later centuries, when the industry producing it had changed.

Thus only in part can the appearance in antiquity of a Greek sanctuary be deduced from what is now visible. Where the major monuments—the temples in particular— are sufficiently upstanding something of the original effect can be experienced by visiting the present remains. Even this can be misleading; no temple is perfectly preserved, and the setting has usually altered to a very considerable extent. Thus

25

photographs of temples, though essential to illustrate their details as buildings, cannot record their function, religious or visual, in the context of the sanctuary. In other sanctuaries, even the temples have suffered such severe destruction that they present nothing of their former appearance at all. Sometimes the ruin is so complete that the plan of the building can be traced not by any surviving structure, but by the cuttings left in the rock on which the foundations were placed. Even more does this apply to the lesser buildings, where total destruction is not unusual. Fortunately, even when a building is totally demolished, fragments of its masonry may still survive. Since Greek architecture adhered to close rules of proportion and standard forms, often these broken pieces of stone may provide a reasonable clue to the original appearance of a building, making a reconstruction, at least on paper, more feasible. Such reconstructions are more valuable in assessing the real appearance of the sanctuary, but it must be remembered that they often incorporate guesses, and are best regarded as approximate guides.

A final advantage of studying the sanctuaries through reconstructed drawings rather than photographs is that it makes it possible to see them at different stages of development. Where the earlier stages are concealed below later development, where the earlier temples are overlain by a final and more massive structure, nothing of the earlier normally remains visible. Excavation beneath the late building may well reveal enough of it to permit a theoretical restoration, if only in part. This, in turn, depends on the perceptiveness and accuracy of the archaeologist who made these discoveries, for once the excavation has been completed it is usually necessary to fill back the trenches, concealing once more the early evidence. Nowhere can it be demonstrated that our knowledge of a sanctuary is anywhere near complete; but some understanding is always possible, beyond the often disjointed appearance of the ruins which survive.

3 The buildings

Temples

The temple is obviously the building which normally dominates the sanctuary, and forms a visual focus for it, even though the ritual depended rather on the altar. Its position in the sanctuary would therefore appear to have been a matter of some importance, and it is surprising to find certain sanctuaries where this is obviously not so, as well as others in which it is by no means clear that the temple is in a carefully planned position. The earliest buildings which can be safely identified as temples—and which stand at the head of an unbroken sequence of development leading to the definitive buildings of the fifth century and later—belong to the eighth century BC, and may indicate an innovation of religious practice of that time. Areas set aside for cult purposes must have existed before that time, and the inference therefore is inevitably that the temple did not come first in the development of the sanctuaries; consequently, it is hardly surprising to find sanctuaries in which the temple does not appear to come first in the architectural arrangement. At Olympia, for example, the focal point of the sanctuary appears to have been the great ash altar, and it is not difficult to conceive a period when this essentially non-architectural feature was the only artificial structure in the entire sacred area. Indeed, it is possible that for a substantial time even the offerings were scanty, the essentially perishable offering of animal sacrifice being of basic importance. Then, when the temple structure was first developed there, it perforce stood to one side. This arrangement is also implicit in the function of a temple buiding, where it was intended to enable the cult-statue it contained to look out to the altar and the sacrifices there performed; like the human spectators, it was placed opposite the altar.

The earliest temples were very small; and so the discrepancy in size between the altar as a central feature (whether a pile of ash or a built structure) and the functionally subordinate but visually dominant temple did not arise. The anomaly was felt, naturally enough, when the temples became much larger, and in sanctuaries which developed later during the period of monumental temple architecture or in an older sanctuary where some re-arrangement was possible, the temple comes more and more to assume the central role in the plan which its form and splendour naturally demands. The culmination of these tendencies appears in the regularly planned sanctuaries of the Hellenistic age, such as that of Artemis Leukophryene at Magnesia, where the temple is more or less at the centre of a regular colonnaded court.

The first temples took the form of small huts, longer than they were wide, and with their side walls extended forward to form a porch, generally with two wooden posts between the side walls, at the front. Such a building occurs in the sanctuary of Hera at Perachora; there it had an apse in place of the rear wall, and measured about 25 by 18 feet (7.62 by 5.49 metres). Other early temples are rectangular, with varied arrangements for the porch, but essentially of similar dimensions. The materials from which they were built were equally simple, selected but unworked stone for the footings, unbaked mud brick for the walls, the posts and beams of treetrunks and branches, with probably a minimum of working, roofs of reed thatch. An alternative system of roofing, used particularly in Crete, and possibly the Aegean islands, was to spread clay on a flat support of poles. Models of such temples placed in the sanctuary of Perachora[1] may indicate that the surfaces of the walls were stuccoed and given painted decoration, even on the exterior. The plan of such temples is essentially that of the great hall in the Bronze Age palaces, and it is often referred to as a *megaron* plan, megaron being the word used by Homer for the great hall of the palaces he describes in his epics. From this follows the assumption that because of the similarity of plan the temple is derived essentially and directly from the great halls of the Bronze Age palaces; but this implies that there was some continuity of construction from the end of the thirteenth century, when the palaces were mostly destroyed, or at least that there was sufficient of them still standing some four centuries later when the temples were built. Both arguments seem unlikely, and it is safer (if less satisfying to those who want to bridge the gulf between the Bronze Age and the classical era) to suppose that the temple plan was simply that of the contemporary simple hut dwelling traditional to the primitive Greeks; and that the great hall of the palaces, like the temples, was a sophisticated development from this same original. If so, a possible argument would be that the Greeks developed the idea of the cult-image (perhaps as an inheritance of the figurines from the late Bronze Age, perhaps because they began to learn of such images elsewhere with the redevelopment of overseas trading contacts) and with it the concept that such an image required its own house; and that this was then modelled on the houses then used by them in their towns and villages.

This Greek revival brought with it the possibility of greatly increased wealth, at least to certain enterprising or favourably placed localities, and, probably, to favourably placed individuals. There was a compelling need, given the dominant role of the gods in Greek society, to pay at least some of the benefits thus received to them. Individual offerings of bronze and other metal, or of terracotta, became much more numerous, and there is here an obvious incentive to the improvement of the temple, both in size and quality of construction. At the same time, there was no pressing need to change the essential plan of the temple as a simple rectangular room with a porch, since this still solved—and would continue to solve—the functional requirements of the building. Thus, with developments in the form of the Greek house away from the concept of the one-room hut to a more elaborate structure with a number of rooms placed round a central enclosed court, the temple by retaining the essential plan of the primitive hut ceased to be recognizable as a house, but became a distinct architectural type in its own right, with its own criteria of design.

The stages of development from the simple hut are largely hypothetical because of the dearth of reliable archaeological evidence. It would seem that it occurred with great rapidity, taking at the most a century, from the middle of the eighth to the middle of the seventh century BC. The obvious way to make the temples more impressive was to increase their size. This created construction problems, for the mud brick used in building the walls is not good weight-bearing material. An increase in the width of the temple (more imposing than a mere increase in length) inevitably required more substantial timbers, beams and rafters for the roof. An obvious device

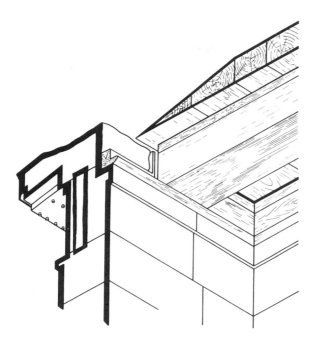

3 Junction of roof and wall, showing the wall-crown (after A. T. Hodge)

was to place a sleeper beam along the top of the mud brick, thus securing a completely even distribution of the weight; that this was done (none, of course, survives) is proved by the representation of such a beam in the crowning course of the stone walls in the later temples, where it was not a structural necessity (fig. 3).[2] It is probable that even the earliest temples employed this form of construction. The next stage of development was to provide upright wooden posts to support these beams, either embedded in the wall, or standing in a row outside it. There is evidence for the provision of such posts within the wall at the temple of Artemis Orthia in Sparta[3] (timber-laced construction of this sort was frequently employed in the late Bronze Age, and the technique may be a survival, rather than a new invention). A row of external post supports is first found in the very large temple built for Hera at her sanctuary on the island of Samos.

It is this Samian temple that appears to be in the forefront of Greek architectural development. The site was successively built over, and the evidence for the earliest structures is thus a little uncertain. The first large temple there was built in the eighth century (perhaps not as early as 800 BC, the date assigned to it by the excavators). This temple is over a hundred feet long; and since the variable Greek feet are not vastly different from the English foot, it seems reasonable to suppose that the intention was to create a length of a hundred feet. Such a temple was of stupendous length compared with structures such as that at Perachora, and it is hardly surprising that the Greeks coined a special word for these outstanding buildings; they are called *hekatompeda*, 'hundred footers', a term intended as a general indication of colossal size rather than a precise measurement. The existence of such a word probably indicates that the development from small to large was very sudden, without gradual, intermediate stages of development. At Samos this was achieved solely by extending the length; the width was only twenty-one feet. Such a building did not require more sophisticated building techniques. There was a central row of wooden posts to help support the roof, but probably nothing more. Long, narrow proportions of this sort are found in early temples at Hermione, and survive even in the later temples of Boeotia. Their existence is also implied by some of the later stone temples of Sicily (fig. 4).[4] The Samos temple was subsequently given the external supports for the roof; it is likely that the original roof required renewal, and that either the walls were damaged, and deemed incapable of supporting the weight of the roof, or it was decided that an external row of supports would give the building greater width, so making it even more impressive. Since the posts are not placed close to the walls it seems that this consideration was uppermost in the minds of their constructors.

The date at which these posts were added is not certain, but probably occurred around 700 BC. It is not unlikely that a similar long narrow temple was constructed at about the same date on the great terraced platform of the sanctuary of Argive Hera, between Argos and Mycenae; but it is not clear whether or not at this time it was given a surrounding colonnade of wooden posts. That it possessed such a colonnade by about 670 BC is a distinct probability. Thus the early seventh century saw the essential development in the form of the major temples from the simple rectangular hut with a porch through the elongated hut to the full temple form, preserving the hut in its more elongated form but surrounding it with an external colonnade, partly for structural reasons, partly to make the temple a more impressive building.

The next stage in the development of temples came with the inevitable improvement in building materials inspired by the knowledge of the more substantial methods employed in other parts of the eastern Mediterranean. There are two aspects of this, apparently synchronous; the development of terracotta roofing tiles; and the employ-

ZEUS, SYRACUSE

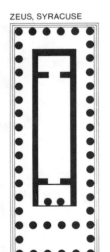

SELINUS, 'C'

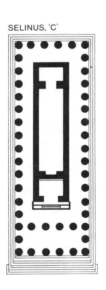

SELINUS, 'D'

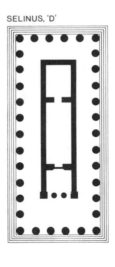

SELINUS, 'FS'

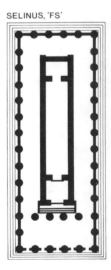

4 Plans of Sicilian temples

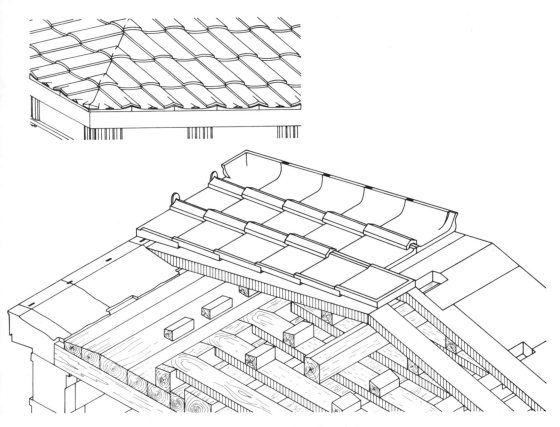

5 Different types of roof tile: above, the archaic temple, Isthmia (after
W. B. Dinsmoor, Jnr) and the Treasury of the Athenians, Delphi (after
A. T. Hodge)

ment of stone masonry construction. The development of a more permanent and
durable form of roofing was essential if the Greek temple was to achieve real monumentality. The reed thatch previously used would require constant renewal, and
without continual and careful attention the simple mud-brick temples must have had
a very short life. There are no signs of tiles from the temples of the eighth century
BC; their introduction belongs to the seventh century, but probably just after the
enlargement of the more important temples. It is not possible to attribute their
invention to any one Greek community, and it is probable that the idea was introduced to Greece from outside, possibly from Anatolia. But the development was particularly associated with the principal trading cities of the seventh century, Corinth
above all and the other cities of the Peloponnese. There are two main categories:
wide flat tiles with turned-up edges (pan-tiles), combined with narrow ridged (or
perhaps curved) cover tiles which span the joints between the edges, a form of tiling
particularly associated with Corinth; the other type consists of curved tiles of equal
widths placed on their backs and over the joints between them, a type associated with
the Spartan territory of Laconia (fig. 5). The second type is obviously the simpler

31

to make, but requires more frequent support, and would need to be bedded in clay. The first type rests on rafters spaced at the width of the pan-tiles, and does not require a clay bedding. All these tiles were of a quite substantial thickness, and consequently of considerable weight; they therefore required much stronger support than the old thatch roofs, and it was now out of the question that they could in any way be supported directly by the mud-brick walls. Because they were to all intents and purposes impervious to rain they did not require to be pitched as steeply as the older roofs; with the adoption of tiled construction the angle of slope of the roof was lowered to about fourteen or fifteen degrees (in place of perhaps fifty or sixty) with a profound effect on the appearance of the building.[5] Another consequence resulted from the fact that tiles are less easily fitted above curved walls (the Perachora temple not only had an apse at one end, but curved side walls as well). Apsidal buildings are thus uncommon; and though it was possible to turn the line of a tiled roof through ninety degrees to give a hipped roof, such construction requires special arrangements at the angles, both of tiling and, particularly, of the wooden framework supporting the tiles. Some early tiled temples did have hipped roofs (the temple of Poseidon at Isthmia, for example, and the early temple of Hera at Foce del Sele, near Paestum in Italy)[6] but this type of roof generally died out, for temples at least, in favour of the simple two-sided ridged roof, terminating in a gable-pediment at either end. Terracotta tiles, normally of the Corinthian type, were used for temples throughout the classical era; exceptionally fine temples, such as the Parthenon on the Athenian Acropolis, used tiles carved from solid marble but in the shape and forms of terracotta. The use of terracotta was not confined to the utilitarian roofing tiles. The special covering tiles along the ridge were often given decorative finials, and the openings otherwise revealed at the bottom of the roof between each row of pan-tiles were concealed behind decorative 'antefixes'. Terracotta was also employed as decorative sheathing in front of rafter ends, and in general over exposed woodwork. In the seventh and sixth century this decorative terracotta work was often most elaborate. It was particularly favoured in the west, in Sicily and southern Italy, where it achieved the heights of elaboration; from here the taste was acquired by the Etruscans, and passed by them to the early architecture of Rome.

Proper stone construction had been practised in Greece during the late Bronze Age, where carefully fitted, squared masonry was used particularly in the great *tholos* (circular) tombs.[7] It is unlikely that such construction continued in Greece during the subsequent dark age, and no trace of any has been found. Squared fitted stone first recurs in a Greek context in the facing of the fortifications of Old Smyrna, of the eighth century BC, perhaps as a result of Anatolian influence.[8] It was not used in the Greek peninsular, and the terrace built for the temple of the Argive Heraion about 700 BC, though employing very massive blocks of stone, does not shape or fit them closely to each other. Such walls do demonstrate that the Greeks were capable of building in stone, where necessary; but they were not yet generally skilled masons, and they did not consider these methods suitable for free-standing buildings. By 650 BC, however, some cities had made the crucial move to stone construction for temples. Here overseas influence seems to be of paramount importance, particularly when, about that time, the Greeks became better acquainted with Egypt, where the great public buildings and temples of stone construction contrasted with the mud

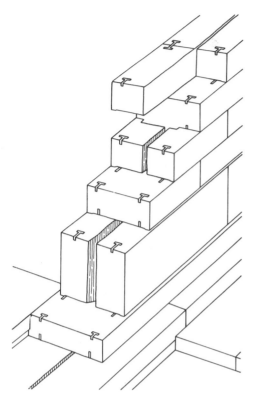

6 Wall of a Greek temple, showing a typical arrangement of the blocks

brick used abundantly in private houses and other humbler structures. Even so, the idea that the all important temple buildings should be constructed not only to a superior size but of superior materials could be one which the Greeks originated for themselves, without direct reference to any specific (as opposed to general) outside influence.

In this also Corinth seems to have played the leading role. Very little survives of the first temple of Apollo, built actually in the city of Corinth about the middle fo the seventh century, and replaced after little more than a hundred years. There is much more of the contemporary temple built by the Corinthians to Poseidon at the sanctuary of Isthmia, a short distance from Corinth, and which survived until about the time of the Persian invasion in 480 BC. This had stone walls (but with wooden columns) and terracotta tiles arranged to form a hipped roof. The excavators found traces of what they believed to be the scaffolding, holes in the ground round the temple to support the scaffolding poles. These have not been found elsewhere, either because other temples have not been investigated so scrupulously and meticulously as at Isthmia; or perhaps because the scaffolding here was particularly massive, in view of the new stone construction techniques.

The forms of these new stone temples, which do not become at all common until the sixth century, reflect in many of their details the earlier construction methods in mud brick, timber, and terracotta; the temple at Isthmia has raised panels on its side walls not found in later temples, which seem to be a translation of the pattern created in mud-brick walls by embedded timber supports. The detailing of the superstructure above the columns, which is not capable of explanation in terms of stone construction, must reflect the patterns created by the various techniques of fitting wood to wood, and to the attachment of terracotta sheathing.[9] The wall crowning member has already been mentioned as a probable vestige of wooden techniques. In later times, the further translation of wooden elements into stone form is clearly attested; for example the ceiling beams and the coffered ceilings they support, at times still made of wood (particularly over the relatively wide spans of the interior room), but at times made of stone (the ceiling between the outer colonnades and the walls). Even so, not all the peculiarities of Greek stone temple architecture can be attributed to wooden prototypes. The walls, for example, are rarely built of simple ashlar courses of equal dimensions for their entire height. It is usual to give the wall a more elaborate footing, comprising three parts, socle, large rectangular slabs set on edge (*orthostats*) and a covering course (fig. 6). This three-fold system is often used in walls where it is the only part constructed in stone, the superstructure above this being of mud brick. A variant occurs in the temple of Hera at Olympia, of the early sixth century BC, again leading to a mud-brick superstructure. Yet this cannot be explained as a convention originating in mud-brick walls, for the orthostats cannot have had any mud-brick equivalent. The probable origin of this device has now been revealed, in a temple built in the Phoenician town of Kition in Cyprus of the ninth century BC, which employs large orthostat slabs; but even these are of earlier origin, for in constructing this building the Phoenicians appear to have been reusing material, in its original arrangement, from another building on the same site, dating from the closing years of the late Bronze Age.[10]

In stone temples the problem of origin is important not only for the technique, but for the differing forms that became established in different regions of the Greek world. Some features were obviously translated from wooden prototypes, but this is not the full explanation. There are two main forms, the Doric, so called because it originated in the Dorian speaking part of Greece, probably Corinth, and not because it was in any way restricted to the Dorian area (plate 2); and the Ionic, which originated in the Ionian region of east Greece (there is a variant but related form used in the Aeolic area just to the north—plate 3). In both the essential arrangements of the temple are the same, the rectangular room (or *cella*, a Latin term) and a porch (*pronaos*) in front, in major temples surrounded by a colonnade (peripteral temples). There are obvious variations in the precise arrangement of the plan; some temples have deep porches, others may have additional false porches at the rear (false, because they do not lead to an actual door giving access to the temple) but the essential ingredients are always there, in Doric and Ionic alike. The principal differences occur in the forms of the columns employed, and the details of the superstructure, or entablature, which they support, but even here the essential elements are common to both; columns with shaft and capital (Ionic also has a separate base), and an entablature consisting of architrave (main beam) surmounted by a frieze and cornice. The details, of course, differ, but the structural function or origin is the same.

In the column, the major difference is the form of the capital. That of the Doric column is essentially circular in plan, a saucer shape, in which the *echinus* (later becoming higher, with straighter sides, and so more resembling a bowl) supports a square bearing element, the *abacus*. The Ionic capital also has an echinus, but partly conceals it behind a pair of volutes to either side, linked by a bolster section at the sides from front to back. The abacus over this is flatter than in Doric, and rectangular rather than square. It has been thought that the Doric capital is essentially a woodworking type, and derives from similar capitals, depicted in frescoes rather than surviving in their original form, in the palaces of Bronze Age Crete and the mainland.[11] However, its re-introduction into Greece, in the eighth century, rather than its continuous survival should be considered as a possibility since such capitals could not have been used with the scanty supports in eighth-century buildings such as the Perachora temple. The idea of capitals with pairs of volutes is definitely of Eastern origin, for they are found not only by the doorways of Cypriot tombs but also on the ivory carvings found in abundance in Assyria although essentially of Syria and Phoenician origin or at least craftsmanship.[12]

Of the entablatures, the *architrave* is in origin essentially the beam, originally wooden, which ran immediately over the columns to stabilize the structure and enable more roof beams than columns to be employed. No sophisticated theory of derivation is needed here. The *friezes* above the architraves are more complex. The Doric consists of alternating vertically grooved sections (the *triglyphs*) and the flat sections (the *metopes*). It is generally supposed that the triglyphs represent beam ends, the metopes the spaces between, filled in wooden architecture with terracotta plaques, examples of which have survived. There are problems caused by this explanation, and the origin of the triglyph is much disputed.[13] In developed stone architecture the beams always occur on a higher level than the triglyphs, coming behind the cornice; it is difficult to see why they were elevated to this position if they were originally at the lower level in wooden architecture. There is also a problem caused by the fact that it is an invariable rule of Doric architecture that at the corners the entablatures must end with triglyphs, which thus would represent an impossible juxtaposition of beam ends. In Ionic architecture the frieze consists of much smaller plain projecting rectangles (called *dentils* because they resemble a row of teeth) with spaces of almost equal size between. These give much more the appearance of beam ends; in certain tombs in Lycia (a non-Greek region of southern Asia Minor) round-ended elements are used in this position, most closely recalling untrimmed branches used in the place of squared beams.[14] The answer is probably that in Doric and Ionic the triglyphs and dentils are intended to recall rafter rather than beam ends, in which case the corner triglyphs are the adjacent visible faces of the angle rafter used in hipped rather than pedimental roofs. Even so, the design of grooving on the triglyphs is elaborate, and is unlikely to be something employed in the unsophisticated temples of the eighth century; that it was used in the more elaborate wooden entablatures of the seventh and sixth centuries (such as once existed on the temple of Hera at Olympia) is virtually certain.

Similar decorative designs—grooved rectangles alternating with squares—are also found on the Syrian ivory carvings, where they form a border pattern for figured scenes, and it is not impossible that an enterprising architect of the early seventh century borrowed the idea for embellishing the first large Greek temples.[15] It is very clear that other purely sculptural or painted patterns—palmettes, lotus buds, alternating lotus and palmette, guilloche (cable) patterns and so forth—which are used with great frequency in Greek architecture (as in other branches of Greek art) are of Near Eastern origin and were introduced to Greece where they occur, for example, in vase decoration in the late eighth and seventh centuries BC. The exact application of these and other sculptured patterns forms an important variation between Doric and Ionic, concealing but not denying the essentially unified structural origin of the two orders of Greek architecture.

The elaboration of design was not confined to the strictly architectural features. The terracotta metope panels used in wooden Doric temples were given painted decoration, figure scenes with border patterns. With the adoption of stone architecture, carved stone decoration was required, and this was extended from the repetitive pattern designs to the use of relief sculpture, on the metopes and in the pediments, and so to full free-standing sculpture. By the middle of the sixth century sculpture in the round was common (but not invariable) for pediment designs; though the sculpture was always placed against the wall of the pediment (the *tympanum*) so that it in fact gave the effect of high relief. Completely free-standing sculpture was restricted to the roof, figures or plant sculptures being used at the three angles of the roof over the pediments; these are known as the *acroteria*. Other forms of sculptural decoration can be found in Ionic temples of the sixth century: continuous relief friezes on the vertical faces of the high parapet gutters which run the length of the buildings over the cornices. The temple of Artemis at Ephesos also had relief figure scenes carved on the bottom drums of selected columns, either of the façade or in the deep porch. Parts of these have survived, and bear inscriptions which proclaim that they were the gift of the wealthy Lydian king, Croesus.

With the translation into stone the definitive forms were established. Later variations in temple architecture consist of the refinement of established details, and particularly the modification of dimensions. Some development occurred in the selection and availability of building materials. Early stone architecture generally had been achieved in the locally available stones, preferably limestone. Some Greek communities were fortunate in possessing local quarries of good-quality white marble, and this became the most favoured stone, where it was available (coloured marbles, also readily available in Greece, had been used in the late Bronze Age, but were not to return to favour until the Roman period). The main limitation was the cost of transport from the quarry to the sanctuary; transport by sea was relatively cheap, and the fine crystalline marble of the island of Paros in the central Aegean was widely used, though principally for sculptural decoration and other details rather than the main construction. Certain limestones were also transported; Athens quarried good-quality limestone from the Piraeus and the district of Eleusis, and some of this was used, for example, at Epidauros on the other side of the Saronic gulf (other stone used there came from Corinth). The most spectacular and important development in this respect was the opening of the marble quarries in Attica, on Mount Pentelicus, which enabled the Athenians to build completely in marble the temples and other major public monuments of the fifth century BC, both before the Persian invasion of 480, and, most important of all, the great building programme of the Periclean age, from 450 to 431; but even here two important temples, at

Sounion and at Rhamnous, situated at some distance from the Pentelicus quarries and (perhaps more significantly) behind that mountain, had to make do with inferior partly discoloured marbles from local quarries.

Another important practice affecting the appearance of the temples in their finished state, and not so readily recognizable in their present ruined form, was the modification of the stone surface by the addition of coats of stucco and painted decoration. Stucco was possibly used to coat and protect the surfaces of mud-brick walls; its extension to stone buildings enabled Greek architects to disguise inferior stone. Classical stucco reaches a very high quality, and the inclusion of powdered marble enabled surfaces not too different in appearance from those of marble structures to be achieved. It was also the custom, even on marble buildings, to pick out certain details in red and blue, and to add decorative patterns in both colours to mouldings and other emphatic surfaces; most of this has irretrievably faded though much was noted by the Victorian architect F. C. Penrose[16] in his study of the Parthenon (though, through fading, he was led to believe that the blues were in fact green). The use of colour decoration was a feature principally of Doric architecture. Ionic seems to have preferred carved detail and patterning. It is possible that the backgrounds to the relief friezes were coloured, probably dark blue, to make the figures stand out more, in the manner of fifth-century vase painting which left the figures light against a black background. In the Erechtheion on the Athenian Acropolis this effect was achieved by pegging figures carved separately in white marble against a background of dark Eleusinian limestone, but this idea was not taken up by other architects.

By the fifth century, then, temples had become imposing buildings, often of substantial size, and dominating the sanctuaries in which they stood not only by their magnitude but by the splendour and elaboration of their decoration, for which they were particularly admired, and by the correctness of their proportions. The Ionic temples achieved some elegance of detail, particularly admirable in the smaller examples, but in the major temples this was often outweighed by the sheer size and bulk of the building and the massive roof. Doric temples made little pretence to elegance, though the need to achieve harmonious and balanced proportions was appreciated; but these temples impressed by their sturdy solidity, giving an appearance of strength, durability and permanence in the face of the less substantial ordinary buildings of the city, an impression appropriate to the cults of the gods, and so often justified by the fact that these are the buildings, in sanctuary and city alike, which have survived.

Altars

The altar of a Greek sanctuary was essentially a raised place on which a fire could be kindled during the festival, and the burnt offerings made to the gods. As we have seen, there was no need for it to achieve a monumental form. With the development of stone architecture, and the introduction of more elaborate embellishment to the buildings of the sanctuaries, it was only natural that the altar, the focal point of ritual within the sanctuary, should follow suit. The chronology of its development has not been elucidated as satisfactorily as that of the temple, but there is no reason to doubt that it did not much lag behind; the important types can be recognized in the sixth century BC. At the same time it must be pointed out that, on the whole, altars are not as well preserved as temples, and there are certain important gaps in our knowledge. For example, we do not know much about the altar of Athena on the Athenian Acropolis, apart from its approximate position and that, as literary references prove and as might be expected, it was already there in the seventh century BC.[17]

Sanctuary altars were usually rectangular in plan (there is a circular one in front of the temple of Apollo, Didyma); smaller altars were often square. The larger examples often stood on a podium, and some required flights of steps for the officiating priest to reach their upper surface. The junction between the podium and the main block of the altar would be decorated with mouldings; there would be other mouldings at the top. On the upper surface there might be low balustrade sections, intended to keep the fire in place. Other embellishment was possible, but on the whole the altars remained simple and rather plain. A particularly ornate type developed in the area adjacent to Corinth in the archaic period, in which the vertical surfaces of the main block were decorated with alternating triglyphs and plain metopes, indicating, it would seem, that the origin of this pattern is strictly a matter of decoration, whatever the reason for its choice as the frieze form for Doric temples. It is interesting that these triglyph altars evolve in the same region, apparently, as the Doric temple. Examples of them are found at Corinth itself, at Perachora, at the Argive Heraion, and in Argos itself, from the sanctuary of Apollo by the agora. Argos also possessed, in the sanctuary of Apollo Pythaios, an altar of plainer type adorned with mouldings only.[18]

The most spectacular altars belong to the Hellenistic age, when elaborate attempts were made to embellish them with columns. Two of these belong to the east Greek world, at Priene and at Pergamon. It is possible that earlier altars in the east Greek area had already achieved some degree of monumentality; the foundations of the altar in front of the temple of Artemis at Ephesos indicate that it was already large in the seventh century BC, before the first truly monumental temple; but its exact appearance is quite uncertain. The Hellenistic great altar of Zeus on the acropolis at Pergamon is the most elaborate of all.[19] It is an independent altar, with no temple attached to its sanctuary. It stands on a five-stepped plinth which is almost square, measuring 119 feet 6 inches by 112 feet 2 inches (36.44 metres by 34.20 metres). Set immediately on the top step, with mouldings top and bottom, is a plain vertical section, similar to smaller altars elsewhere, but here serving only as a substructure for something much more elaborate. It is interrupted for the central sixty feet of the west side by a continuation of the flight of steps, here rising to a total number of twenty-seven. Elsewhere, the plain section carries a much taller vertical, again with elaborate mouldings top and bottom; but this section, far from being plain, is decorated with the grandiose series of sculptures in high relief depicting the struggle of gods and giants. This in turn is surmounted by an Ionic colonnade, twenty-one columns on the east, north and south sides, four on either flank of the west side, six along the return to the top of the steps, and fourteen at the top of the flight of steps. Behind these were smaller Ionic columns on tall plinths, leading to the central open paved rectangle. This should have been surrounded by more colonnades, but it appears that these were never completed. In this court was the sacrificial altar; on the walls of the court, another relief frieze depicting the story of Telephus. The altar was constructed in the time of Eumenes II, King of Pergamon from 197 to 159 BC. It was probably left unfinished at his death.

This altar is obviously rather more than the functional altar at the centre of its court; the elaborate architectural frame here takes the place of a sanctuary, and even of the temple. Earlier examples occur of an embellished setting for an altar. At Perachora, for example, the triglyph altar was subsequently placed in a sort of baldachino, formed by eight Ionic columns.[20] This, significantly, stood in front of a temple. Another embellished setting for an altar was created in the agora at Athens for the altar of the twelve gods. Here a surrounding stone fence was apparently decorated with relief slabs to either side of openings in the east and west sides; but of the form of the altar itself next to nothing is known.

In the west Greek area a monumental altar was constructed at Syracuse by King Hiero in the third century BC.[21] This was formed by extending the long narrow rectangular altars such as that in the Argive Heraion to altogether fantastic length. Its dimensions are 633 feet 7 inches by 51 feet 6 inches (193.12 metres by 15.70 metres).

Gateways

Some—but by no means all—sanctuaries marked the passage from outside by an elaborate formal gateway; others had less spectacular entrance barriers, designed to protect the sanctuary from unwanted intruders, while some did not find it necessary to put up any barriers at all. The elaborate gateways were invariably in the form of an outer and inner porch, separated by a wall with one or more doorways. The Greek term for such a structure is *propylon*, or the plural form *propylaia*, which means rather a 'gateway complex' and is used for the extremely complex structure at the entrance to the Athenian Acropolis. The existence or lack of such a gateway is not dependent on the importance of the sanctuary; it is noticeable that there was no elaborate gate-structure at Olympia, at least until Roman times, or at Delphi.

The type has an interesting history, for it is found in the palaces of Bronze Age Crete, at Knossos, and in the palaces of the late Bronze Age of the mainland. The problems this raises are similar to those of the relationship between the halls of the Bronze Age palaces and the classical temples; for, as with the temples, it is unlikely that any of the Bronze Age gateways survived in recognizable form the holocausts at the end of the thirteenth century BC; and there is no evidence for continuity of type through the intervening dark age. Yet their functions are the same. It could perhaps be argued that the similarity of form is a coincidence, architects at widely separated periods of time devising independently the same solution to the same architectural problem; that in both instances the idea of setting a porch in front of a door derives from the similar treatment of the entrance to rooms, whether of palace or temple. On the other hand this explanation cannot be applied to the additional, inward-facing 'porch' behind the door. The propylon type is not the natural solution to the requirement for a functional entrance, designed simply to keep people out; in the Bronze Age, there is a noticeable contrast between the entrance gate through the fortifications at Tiryns—massive door jambs either side of equally massive walls, and with doors that were fixed with wooden bars—and the two inner gateways to the outer court and inner court, which are of the columnar propylon type. At

Athens the Acropolis propylon, built originally in the sixth century BC, occupies the
position of a military-type entrance of the late Bronze Age, similar to the entrance
gate at Tiryns and the Lion gate at Mycenae. Thus at both periods there is the same
distinction between a functional and a monumental entrance; and it does not seem
impossible that the concept and form of the monumental entrances was somehow
transmitted through the dark age from the Bronze Age to the classical. How, and
where, this happened must remain uncertain; in this context, it should perhaps be
noted that the earliest post-Bronze Age monumental propylon would appear to
be the seventh century BC example at the sanctuary of Hera on the east Greek island
of Samos.

Despite its ornamental appearance, and the addition of other rooms and colonnades round its central, gateway section, the Athenian propylaia forms an effective
barrier. Once all five of its doorways were shut, it was impossible to enter the Acropolis. The predecessor of the Periclean propylaia was defended (admittedly, un-
successfully) against armed assault by the Persians during their occupation of Athens
in 480 BC. This was because the Acropolis, besides being a religious sanctuary (a
function which certainly dominated it in the fifth century) was also a fortified citadel,
and for long the only fortified part of Athens, the town at its foot probably not
receiving its ring wall until the fifth century. Sanctuaries which were purely religious
in character and location did not, at least under stable conditions, require the same
degree of physical security. Flanked by demarcation boundaries rather than walls
the gateway could not act as an effective barrier. In such sanctuaries gateway buildings
were not functionally necessary. The fact that they do occur—examples can be seen
at the sanctuary of Asklepios at Epidauros, the sanctuary of Herakles on the island of
Thasos and, outside the Greek world, but built under Greek architectural influence,
at the Carian sanctuary of Zeus at Labraunda[22]—demonstrates that they had become
desirable embellishments for sanctuaries. The propylon at Epidauros acknowledges
its inability to serve as a barrier in an unwalled sanctuary by dispensing with the cross
wall and door, and consists simply of a rectangular porch structure with colonnades
at front and back. From this and similar gateways it is clear that the most important
function of these structures was to act as an imposing entrance rather than a barrier,
to make clear to those approaching the sanctuary (and perhaps, in particular, the
sacred processions) that they were leaving the secular world and about to enter the
sacred precinct. It thus repeats the architectural rhythm of the entrance to the temple,
where columns between side walls similarly announce that one is approaching a
particularly sacred area; or the splendid porch entrances to the dining-courts, in the
same sanctuary of Asklepios, and again at Thasos. Thus the gateway buildings help
enhance the sense of drama, of movement into and through the sanctuary, and are
important not just for themselves but for the atmosphere they help create, and the
state of mind they inculcate into the person who passes through them.

Other buildings

The religious activity of Greek sanctuaries centred on the fulfilment of ritual obliga-
tions to the gods. These might take the form of the sacrifices offered by the community
to thank the god for his past benevolence and to secure his goodwill for the future;

or the humbler gifts vowed by individuals in return for more personal benefits. The private dedications could be made, in all probability, without fuss and formality; they would not involve anything resembling a religious service. The sacrifices offered by the community, on the other hand, might well be attended by large numbers of people, depending on the importance and location of the sanctuary and its cult; but these would be infrequent affairs, normally restricted to one occasion each year, though at these times the festivities would extend over several days. There were also festivals which were celebrated once every two years, or once every four years, though these were particularly concerned with the addition of athletic and other contests on top of the normal sacrifical ritual; sacrifices were normally needed every year.

For most of the year, the sanctuary would be almost empty of worshippers, given over to the property and possessions of the gods; only at the annual festival would it be crowded. These extremes, inevitably, are reflected in the architectural arrangements; buildings and other structures designed to accommodate the worshippers are less common, and often less substantially constructed, than those concerned with the affairs of the gods. The buildings that are provided for the worshippers are those which give shelter whether from rain, or more likely, the intense heat of the summer sun; buildings where meals could be taken and where sleeping accommodation could be provided. Most sanctuaries had water supplies—indeed, the presence of a spring or other copious supply of water often seems to have determined the siting of a sanctuary—and these might be organized at formal fountain houses. Other specialized structures—theatre and stadium—might be provided where a festival included dramatic or athletic contests, though these normally would be adjacent to the sanctuary, rather than in it; and often contests of this sort were celebrated without the need for formal, architectural accommodation.

Shelter was provided by means of extended colonnades, the *stoas*. Behind the colonnade there was usually a blank wall, but variations which placed the colonnade in front of a line of rooms were possible. Indeed, the architectural forms of the stoas are immensely variable, and it is not possible to give here a succinct account of them which would cover all the permutations available. Anything given in the form of a general rule about them is more than likely to be broken in practice somewhere in the Greek world. Very often, though they provide shelter for the worshippers, they combine this with other functions; for instance, they may house offerings made to the gods for which there is not room in the temple. Their arrangement makes it natural to place them on the borders of the sanctuary, facing inwards. Out of this eventually develops the highly organized sanctuary, in which the boundary is entirely defined by inward facing stoas. Obviously, the contribution made by stoas to the visual appearance of a sanctuary is equally variable; they may be small and insignificant, or extensive and at times more important than the shrine itself. The materials from which they are constructed are variable, with cheaper methods much more frequently employed—timber posts and mud-brick walls, or inferior local and easily quarried stone rather than marble. Where they use the established architectural orders, these are often modified for the sake of economy; Ionic, with its complex carved decoration is rare and externally stoas are normally built in the Doric order even in the east Greek Ionian area, often with wider intercolumnar

41

spacing (so requiring fewer columns) than in the temples. The use of sculpture is rare and restricted; pediments and metopes are left plain. The colonnades are normaly placed on a lower platform than in the temples; one step (or, at the most, two) is common. The floors behind the colonnades are often of beaten earth, rather than paved. The tiles are invariably of terracotta. Stoas, in short, are intended as utilitarian buildings, whose architectural merit is minimal, or merely incidental. Only rarely do they provide a complete frame to the sanctuary or the temple, thus acquiring architectural importance; and even then one senses they were not intended to be admired as buildings, in the sense that the temple obviously was. It is, perhaps, instructive to note here that the geographer Strabo, writing in the first century BC, is enthusiastic about the architectural merits of the temple dedicated to Artemis Leukophryene at Magnesia-on-the-Maeander, but says nothing of the framework of stoas which formed the complete boundary of its precinct.[23]

A more specialized type of building is that generally termed a treasury (a correct translation of the ancient Greek word *thesauros* used to describe them by authors such as Pausanias[24]). These occur in the international sanctuaries, and, despite their name, are more than mere storehouses. They take the form of small non-peripteral temples (plate 4). The buildings themselves, like temples, are offerings to the god erected in the sanctuary by a single city; like a temple they could contain other offerings, but not a cult-statue. Unlike stoas, they are invariably well and solidly built. Some, such as the treasury of the Siphnians at Delphi, are particularly lavish. They are found in the archaic age, and are still being constructed in the fifth century.

The buildings for meals and for sleeping accommodation are more specialized than stoas and much rarer (though they may be included in stoa arrangements). Sanctuaries did not, normally, have permanent residents. So by meals we do not mean the ordinary eating arrangements of people who happen to live in sanctuaries, but the special ritual meals and feasts which often appear an essential part of cult practice. When an animal sacrifice was made, the meat was consumed by the worshippers; in the important festivals large numbers of animals were killed, with only a token offering at the altar, and no provision could have been made to house the worshippers, who attended in their thousands, while they ate. Where special buildings or rooms for dining purposes were constructed in the sanctuaries, the accommodation they provided is limited. It is not possible to tell how the privileged few who were admitted to them, to eat in comfort rather than *al fresco*, were selected. Presumably the choice was made on the basis of dignity; they were city magistrates, or priests, or other people of importance.

At their banquets the ancient Greeks reclined on couches, which were arranged round the sides of a room. There are several features which enable us to detect when rooms were used for this purpose, though they are not necessarily all present in every room so used (plate 5). The floors tend to be raised by an inch or two along the sides, giving a strip just a little wider than the width of the couches which rested on it. The couches followed in sequence, so that the foot of an end couch of those along one wall would be placed in the corner, at the start of the next wall; the couches were not arranged symmetrically, and the space which had to be left for the door (achieved by omitting one of the series of couches along that wall) was invariably off centre.[25] These arrangements are clearly demonstrated in a pair of rooms at the sanctuary of

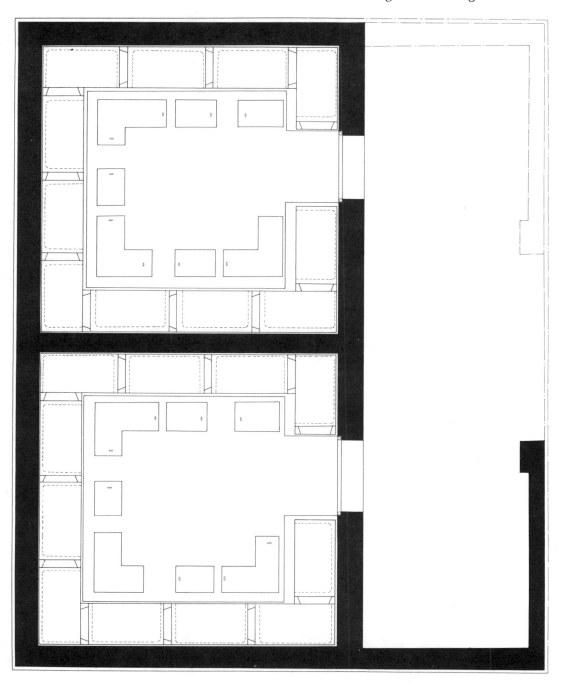

7 Plan of the dining-rooms at Perachora

Hera at Perachora (fig. 7). Here the function of the rooms is proved by the survival of two couches, durably carved from single blocks of stone. The floor is of pebble cement, with a smoother raised strip against the walls, interrupted only at the doorways. The position of the couches is determined by the survivors; there was one to the right of the door, its foot placed in the corner, then three more on the side wall, the last with its foot in the next corner, then another three. Each wall, then, had against it three couches and the foot of a couch from the previous wall; except that one couch was omitted at the entrance. This gives a total of eleven couches, and since they are of regular dimensions, the room was perfectly square, 20 feet 8½ inches by 20 feet 8½ inches (6.32 by 6.32 metres). There are small holes in the cement floor by the couches, into which the legs of wooden tables could be fitted.

It is interesting that rooms of precisely similar dimensions with off-centre doors appear in several other sanctuaries—in Corinth, Epidauros and Athens, for example.[26] Evidence for the couches exists in some of these, but not all; yet it is clear that the arrangement of the rooms is dictated by the need to accommodate eleven couches, and the dimensions by the existence of standard dimensions for the couches themselves. The buildings which can be recognized as those constructed for dining facilities occur in various forms. The Perachora example consists of two rooms side by side, with a long ante-room in front of both. One at Athens consists of four rooms side by side, with a colonnade in front (possibly replacing an original ante-room). At Epidauros the rooms are in a large structure with a central courtyard. This building also contains other, much larger, rooms, and it is clear that these also were used to accommodate couches, in much greater numbers than the select, eleven-couch rooms. Other buildings, less regular in plan and arrangement, may well have functioned as dining-rooms, and these will be noted where they occur. As with the stoas, the structure of the dining-rooms is simpler than that of the temples. Walls may be of mud brick over a stone footing. The cement floors are generally utilitarian, though mosaic floors are not unknown; one of the reasons for the use of cement is undoubtedly to facilitate washing them down after the feasting. The dining-rooms at Perachora were externally rather plain, though columns are used for the façades or courtyards of others. The building at Epidauros has an elaborate ceremonial entrance, with a splendid columnar porch, though the walls of the main structure were of mud brick.

Sleeping accommodation is less easy to recognize; though it must be remembered that the couches in the dining-rooms could equally well function as beds. The need for sleeping accommodation varied. Obviously the city sanctuaries and their festivals would be attended mostly by people who returned to their own homes at night, and visitors could easily find accommodation elsewhere in the city. Sanctuaries which were some distance from the towns which supported them might be attended, at the period of the festival, by large numbers of people who would perforce spend the night in the vicinity. Most, undoubtedly, spent the nights of the festival in the open area, and there are references in the ancient authors to worshippers bringing with them palliasses on which to sleep.[27] The construction of buildings to provide sleeping accommodation (at Olympia, for example) occurs comparatively late in the history of the sanctuaries; and again seems destined for the privileged few; it is, perhaps, the increasing emphasis on social distinctions in the Hellenistic age that made them possible. These buildings are generally arranged around courtyards. That at Olympia stood just outside the perimeter of the sanctuary. Thucydides mentions a large one, on two storeys, built at the sanctuary at Plataea by the Spartans after they had destroyed the city in 427 BC.

In certain sanctuaries, on the other hand, the act of sleeping was part of the ritual; this is particularly true of the healing cult of Asklepios, which required those seeking the god's medicinal aid to pass the night in the sanctuary. In these instances, sleeping accommodation was provided in buildings within the sanctuary. These were not luxurious; large open halls or stoas, in which people would sleep, apparently, on the floor. Again, the forms of structure were utilitarian. Buildings of this nature were not common, and are unimportant in any general assessment of the appearance of sanctuaries.

When the festivals were attended by large numbers of people in the heat of summer, the need for water supplies is obvious. They were also required for ritual purposes, for the acts of cleansing and purification necessary before entering into the divine presence. The organization and conservation of these supplies was, therefore, of considerable importance, and often took the form of architectural structures of some elaboration. These might be inside the area of the sanctuary, or adjacent to it, so that worshippers could purify themselves before entering. In some sanctuaries wells were provided, but a constant flow of cool fresh water was obviously preferable. If possible, sanctuaries were in the vicinity of natural springs, but these would be enhanced artificially. The rock out of which the spring flowed would be opened up, to create sizeable underground chambers, in which quantities of water could be kept penned up. The flow was directed through spouts, usually decorated in the form of lion's heads, into draw basins in front of the rock. Over them shade was provided by roofed structures, often with colonnaded façades (fig. 8). The area in front of the draw basins would be paved, and the resulting structure provided a pleasant amenity (plate 6).[28] On occasions considerable engineering works were undertaken to provide adequate water supplies. At Perachora, which had no natural source of water, an immense storage tank, of unique shape and arrangement, was provided in front of the double dining-room described above, and at another part of the site deep shafts were dug to tap the water table a hundred feet underground, whence the water would be lifted by machinery and fed into storage chambers at the surface, fronted with the usual arrangement of draw basins and colonnaded fountain house. Both these systems appear to date from the early Hellenistic age, about 300 BC (though it may be doubted whether the water-raising machinery for the second system was ever installed).[29] In general, this follows the pattern by which the ancillary structures to the religious sanctuaries became more elaborate in the later period. Indeed, in the Roman period some sanctuaries acquired fountain structures of an overwhelming and excessively elaborate nature; that built by Herodes Atticus at Olympia in the second century AD is an example of this type.

Lesser monuments

So far we have considered the sanctuaries purely in architectural terms; the forms and appearance of buildings that stood in them, and their relationship with each

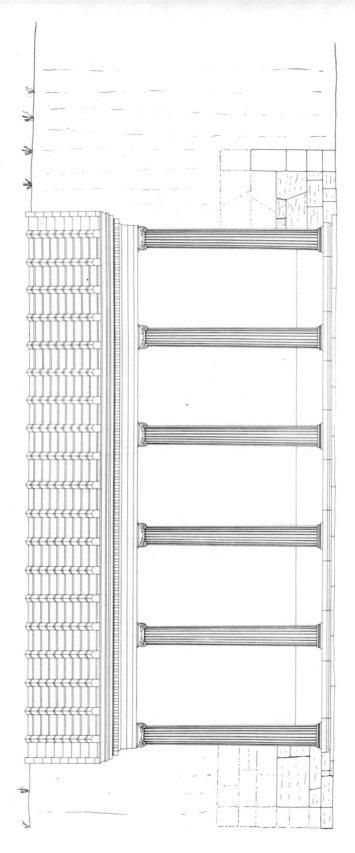

8 The fountain house, Perachora, reconstructed

other. These, as it were, provided the bare bones of the sanctuaries, but they were surrounded by other monuments, not strictly buildings, but of a semi-architectural nature and of course by statuary with its plinths and settings. Here, obviously, the range is enormous, from single statues on simple bases up to commemorative structures and cenotaphs, such as the monument of Philip at Olympia, which are full-size buildings best treated as architecture. Important categories include *exedrai*, stone benches either rectangular or semicircular in shape; and enclosures with groups of statues or other monuments. These were put up for a variety of reasons; private dedications by wealthy individuals, monuments serving the religious purposes of the cities, and erected by them; trophies and other monuments resulting from the successful outcome of war and battles. All, having been put in the sanctuary, were regarded as the possession of the god to whom they had been dedicated, and their removal from the sanctuary was, normally, unthinkable. In the international sanctuaries, states who were bitter enemies might find their monuments standing side by side, protected impartially by the god. The despoiling of sanctuaries was sacrilege, and the action of unprincipled barbarians. Thus the sanctuaries tended to accumulate such monuments with the passing of time, and undoubtedly presented a much more cluttered appearance later in their history than they did at the beginning. Some monuments, it is true, might be overthrown by enemies, earthquakes or other natural disasters and, if they could not be repaired and re-erected, their remains would be discreetly buried but still in the sacred area. Some statues were removed by the Persians during their invasion of Greece and, much more systematically and thoroughly, by the Romans who robbed the Greek sanctuaries to adorn their own cities, old Rome and new Rome alike.

There appears to have been no orderly system, normally, behind the arrangement of these monuments. At Epidauros in the sanctuary of Asklepios there seems to have been a formal square or place in front of the temple, a widening of the approach from the propylon, whose boundary was defined by a series of exedrai regularly and systematically placed; but this was exceptional, and results from the comparatively late and deliberate development of that sanctuary. More usually, the monuments were placed where opportunity arose, leaving clear only the essential areas for human congregation. There was obvious competition for desirable locations, particularly when it was important that the dedication of the monument, or the cause for its dedication, should be seen. Thus, even though there might be no plan, the areas where monuments were put might be reasonably defined. The obvious choices were the vicinity of the temple (many minor dedications might well be placed on the steps of the temple itself) and by the side of the route, or *sacred way* from the gateway to the heart of the sanctuary, the temple or perhaps rather the altar of the principal god.

Sacred ways were the natural routes from the outside to the inside of the sanctuary, and are vital to an understanding of its arrangement. They were not planned in the older sanctuaries; the direct and straight line at Epidauros is again in this respect an indication of its late development. Obviously, if there were no other obstacles, the route ran in a reasonably direct fashion from the entrance to the focal point, as it does at Olympia; but even there it is not obviously related to the shape of the sanctuary and the buildings in it. The entrance probably was determined by the line of the approach from outside the sanctuary, and nothing else. At Delphi, the route is most indirect, forming a complete zig-zag; here the reason is obviously the position of the sanctuary on the hillside, and the need to ease the gradient of the sacred way as much as possible to accommodate the processions and sacrificial victins. Even if the roads themselves did not survive—that at Delphi, for example, was paved—they could be defined by the position of the monuments lining them, as they jostle for the attention of the worshipper. Here untidiness and apparent disorder reigned, in contrast to the careful rhythm and balance of the temples. The arrangement at Epidauros suggests that the incongruity was noticed. Somewhat earlier, when the Acropolis at Athens was reconstructed in the fifth century BC, an attempt was made to create a more direct relationship between the formal entrance, the route into the sanctuary, the altar and the principal temples; but even here the piecemeal arrangement of the minor monuments must soon have distorted the intended symmetry.

9 *Opposite*, Olympia: plan of the sanctuary

4 The financing of sanctuaries

Greek sanctuaries came into being long before the development of coined money, which occurred towards the end of the seventh century BC.[1] With the beginning of stone architecture before that date, the economic implications of the sanctuaries and their construction were already complex. Skilled craftsmen were needed to quarry, shape and fit the stones, and they would need to be requited for their labour. The development of money simplified this problem, and when we begin to find evidence surviving for the financial aspect of the sanctuaries, it can already be expressed in money terms.

The expenses of Greek sanctuaries involved much more than the construction of temples and other buildings. In the account of various sanctuaries which forms the second part of this book, it is possible to see when building programmes were put into effect. During the period when architectural forms were developing towards an accepted standard there was quite frequent replacement of out-of-date buildings. The more perishable nature of the earlier structures again led to replacement, though it is significant to notice that the mud-brick and timber temple of Hera at Olympia survived well into the Roman period (though with its wooden columns replaced one by one by stone) while the even more primitive early temple at the Argive Heraion was still the principal building of that sanctuary at the middle of the fifth century BC. Once a substantial temple had been built it was likely to be replaced only if destroyed by accident (for example, the temple of Apollo at Delphi) or by enemy action (for example, the old temple of Athena on the Acropolis). Exceptionally, if a city became particularly wealthy it might decide to replace an inadequate temple with a more splendid monument. Alternatively, it might create an additional temple, leaving the older one standing. In the fifth century Athens created a series of new temples, where previous temples had been destroyed by the Persians, or where the cult had previously made do without any magnificence. Such a building programme reflects in part the piety and religious attitudes of Athenian society; but it was made possible on that scale only by the fact that Athens was benefiting from her control of an overseas empire, and consequently had the money available. But in general the sanctuaries did not spend, constantly and consistently, large sums of money on building; periods of construction were separated by long periods when building work was in abeyance.

The revenue of the sanctuaries was also needed to provide for the year-to-year functions; above all, the provision of sacrifices, not only the symbolical burnt offerings to the gods, but the meat which was distributed to the worshippers. It may be doubted that much of this necessarily involved cash payment. The animals (or other edibles) which were consumed were more likely to be presented to the sanctuary in kind, by the state or by individuals. Mention has already been made of the fact that the subject allies of Athens had to provide a suit of armour and a cow for each Great Panathenaic festival. Systems of tithing were a means of supporting the cults, possibly in money, but possibly also in agricultural produce which would be used for the sacrifices rather than as a means of supporting a building programme. Such tithes do not seem to have been a universal imposition or annual revenue, as were the tithes in support of the church, but might result from different circumstances. Sometimes the tithe was, in the literal meaning of the English term, a tenth part. Property at Athens confiscated by the state from individuals condemned in the courts for serious political offences was sold, and a tenth part of the proceeds given to Athena, that is, for the protecting cult of the city.[2] Other proportionate sums might be deducted in other places; the cult of Herakles on Thasos received a ninth part of the produce from certain land.[3] The concept of the offering of 'first fruits' to the god is a general one; again at Athens, Athena received as first fruits one sixtieth of the tribute paid by the subject allies to the treasurers of the allied league, and perhaps before the treasury had been moved from Delos to Athens this had been paid to Delian Apollo.[4] Other offerings might be made, by cities and individually, which were useless for the general financing of the cult, precious and valuable objects which had to be kept in the sanctuary. On the whole it is likely that much of the day-to-day running of the sanctuary might be met from offerings made in kind rather than cash, and this was obviously the system necessarily employed before the invention of coin; the primitive system retained some influence even over sanctuaries in later, more sophisticated times.

Nevertheless money was needed, and particularly for building. It was raised by various means, which obviously varied from cult to cult. First came contributions from the state, which went especially to those cults which had a particular interest in, or significance for, the city. Some of these contributions would have been made on a regular basis, the payment of first fruits to Athena at Athens, whether from the tribute of the allies, or from the general income of the state. Others would have come in an irregular and unpredictable way—the tithing of confiscated property, the payment of indemnities by enemies beaten in war, for example when the rulers of Syracuse exacted money from the Carthaginians after their abortive attack in 480, the money being used for the construction of new temples. What is less certain is the extent to which the Greek cities were accustomed to provide money out of their general funds for temple building and other religious activity. It would appear that money was diverted by Pericles for the construction of some, at least, of the fifth-century Athenian temples from funds that should have been used for other purposes.[5] Whatever the accuracy or otherwise of the accusations made about this by his political enemies, it appears at least to have been possible for such allotment of public money to have been made. Other special grants of money might have been made by individuals, either as part of a regular system used, for example, at Athens, whereby the wealthy citizens were called upon to finance various undertakings from their personal wealth, or as a voluntary contribution made to enhance their personal prestige for obvious political purposes.[6] An extension of this concept may be seen in the grants made by the non-Greek King Croesus of Lydia to the building of the sixth-century temple of Artemis at Ephesos, the purpose of which was clearly to win the political support of the Ephesians as well as the religious support of Artemis.

The sanctuaries which were of international importance again expected to receive contributions not only from the often impoverished city in whose territory they were situated, and from local citizens, but principally from the other wealthier cities which patronized their cults. At Delphi, for example, not only was the sanctuary embellished by buildings which were themselves the gift of cities and individuals (the various treasuries, the stoa of Attalos and so forth) but the financing of the temple construction made necessary by land slip and accidental destruction in the sixth and fourth centuries was undertaken partly by individuals, partly by communities. There survives an inscription[7] relating to the fourth-century rebuilding which records these contributions; these range from 3587 drachmai, three-and-a-half obols from the city of Apollonia (described as 'first fruits') down to a mere one-and-a-half obols given by Echeniche of Phleious, and again by Kleonika from the same city (an obol was one-sixth of a drachma). That small individual contributions were collected by sanctuaries is also borne out at the sanctuary of Asklepios in Corinth where a stone collecting box for contributions was prominently placed in front of the temple.

Another important source of revenue which might be devoted to building as well as general purposes came from the property of the cult itself. Landed property was of considerable importance. All states contained areas of sacred land, belonging not to the citizens but to one or other of the gods worshipped there. Though there were taboos on the cultivation of some sacred land (under what circumstances it is impossible to say, but long-established traditions were obviously important here) more often the land owned by the cult was leased out to farmers. The rent, which might take the form of a tithe, was paid to the administrators of the cult. Such rent might be in kind or cash. The more important cults might possess substantial estates, but the identification of these, and their locality in relation to the sanctuary, cannot be generally determined. The cults also acted as banks, lending out sums of money at interest.

Details of such loans again survive recorded on inscriptions.[8] During the three year period from 377 to 374 BC, for example, Apollo of Delos received four talents 3993 drachmai two-and-a-half obols (a talent is six thousand drachmai) as interest on loans paid by ten different cities, all in the immediate neighbourhood of Delos; and interest on loans paid by various private individuals, all from Delos or the neighbouring island of Tenos, totalling 5325 drachmai. This particular inscription is interesting because it appears to give complete financial accounts of Apollo for this period. Other revenue came from confiscated estates 'claimed on the basis of information given', goods seized by distraint and rents from temple lands on Delos and the adjacent island of Rheneia (for a period of two years) and houses on Delos itself (for a period of one year). This amounted to three talents 1326 drachmai, giving a total recorded revenue for the period of eight talents 4644 drachmai two-and-a-half obols. Other information is given on the back of the stone, relating to the full administrative period of four years from 377 to 373 BC. From this we learn that eight cities were in arrears of payment of interest on loans, to a total of seven talents 4246 drachmai three-and-a-half obols, though in addition to these figures part payments had been made; that five talents were owed by three cities which had made no payments at all. There is also a list of private borrowers who had defaulted. We are given the names of eight Delians each fined and banished to perpetual exile for dragging the administrators of the cult out of the temple and striking them. Finally, there are lists of property sacred to Apollo, and including, besides homes, potteries and a smithy. Thus on Delos Apollo acts much as a citizen, engaged in banking and commercial transactions.

The inscription also gives some indication of expenditure; and this is devoted to the requirements of the festivals, rather than building; a crown dedicated to Apollo, tripods as prizes (in the Homeric fashion) to victors in the choral competitions, a talent for the leaders of the sacred embassies (from other Greek cities, principally Athens), one hundred and nine sacrificial oxen, costing one talent 2419 drachmai, gold leaf to gild their horns, fees to the gilder, preliminary sacrifice, fodder for the oxen, customs dues, timber, supplies for the officials of the cult and miscellaneous items such as transport charges. Such an inscription throws much light on the ordinary financial concerns of a major Greek sanctuary; it also demonstrates that building is unlikely to have come from these general funds, except in a minor way; for unless the timber was required for building, the only construction work mentioned is of a wall and the repair of the residence of a 'chairman' (whoever he was).

There is some information about the sums of money required to put up the major religious buildings. Some, particularly in the literary sources, is patently unreliable. When we are told, for example, that the Propylaia at Athens cost two thousand talents, almost three times the whole annual revenue of the state, scepticism is inevitable.[9] More reliable information is found in the actual building records which were durably inscribed on stone; the outstandingly full and informative set from Epidauros have formed the basis of a recent study.[10] There the temple of Asklepios, of the early fourth century BC, and approximately contemporary with the Delian accounts just described, cost somewhat over twenty-three talents, while the gold and ivory cult-statue placed in it cost at least fifty. This temple is not particularly large, and the cost would have increased if it had received more sculptural decoration. The circular building in the same sanctuary, the so-called tholos, which was more elaborate, more highly decorated, and more complicated to construct, cost at least forty and possibly as much as sixty talents. In both these buildings, of course, construction was spread over several years (in the case of the tholos, probably as many as thirty years).

Such figures require careful interpretation, and need to be related to wage levels and the general income of the state. An average wage for a skilled workman would appear to have been in the region of a drachma a day. Assuming that there were about three hundred working days in the year (allowing for festivals and other interruptions) the cost of the temple of Asklepios implies a work force of about fifty men employed for ten years. This includes, of course, costs of quarrying and transport. The number would be reduced by various factors; the cost of particularly valuable material bought in, profit to entrepreneurs, and other incidental costs which cannot be interpreted as wages for day-labourers. The cost in terms of the drain on the resources of the state is much more variable. Here Epidauros is an exception. It was intended to be an international sanctuary, and it is most likely that the greater part of the funds was raised by external contributions. The total cost, of course, was much more than that of the temple alone, for the whole sanctuary with its ancillary buildings was under construction. Even so, the cost was spread out over much of the century, and, with the outside contributions, far from representing a serious drain on the resources of Epidauros, which was only a small place, probably provided a welcome source of employment, at least for labourers (it is likely that a majority of the skilled craftsmen came, like the funds to support them, from other communities).

Normally, a city would be expected to finance its own sanctuaries out of its own resources. The fact that the more powerful cities appear to have more elaborate sanctuaries is an indication that relative wealth and expenditure were important to the building programmes (Sparta, whose financial organization was deliberately kept in a primitive, pre-monetary condition, is the exception that proves the rule, for though powerful, she could not sustain the expenditure on building, and has none of the magnificent temples of the type built by her fifth-century rival, Athens). What proportion of wealth was expended on religious architecture is more problematical. It has been estimated that the Parthenon, built between 447 and 436, and the Propylaia, built between 436 and 431, cost a total of seven hundred talents, or about forty-four talents a year; perhaps a tenth of the Athenian revenue (excluding tribute).[11] Modifications have to be made to this. These two were not the only religious buildings being constructed in this period. On the other hand, we do not know that the tribute should be excluded from these calculations, nor can we assess the contribution from individuals (whose revenue is not included with that of the state) or of the cults themselves. The conclusion to be drawn seems to be that when cities were building temples a high proportion of their revenue was devoted to them; that, in terms of the expenditure on public architecture of all forms, a very high proportion went on religious buildings; but that at the same time, it must be remembered that major spending on religious buildings was intermittent in the extreme, and often separated by very long periods when little or no expense was incurred at all.

The control of religious finances and building programmes is important. Each cult obviously had its own funds and its own administration. There were boards of officials responsible for these. Since the cults were important, not only for their own sake but for the interest and concern they exercised for the state to which they belonged, it was natural for the government of the state also to be concerned with their management. Each cult had its own priests, men or women according to what was established by tradition as appropriate, who were responsible for the performance of the sacrifice; possibly the ritual slaughter of the animal, if an animal sacrifice was customary, certainly the offering of the burnt sacrifice. Priesthoods tended to be restricted to members of particular families, who thus acquired an ancestral interest in religious matters. At Athens, for example, one of the priestly families was that of the Kerykes. They were concerned with the cult of Demeter and Kore at Eleusis, while in political life (in which they did not play a prominent role) they were concerned to see that the state conducted its affairs in accordance with proper religious usage. They were involved in the trial and prosecution of the notorious political leader Alkibiades for sacrilege, and anxious, after he had been exiled for this, to prevent his return to the city, which would involve religious pollution. Such priestly families, however, did not constitute a professional clergy; apart from their priestly duties they lived the normal social, political and economic life of citizens from their class and standing in the cities.

There were in addition to the priests, groups of administrative officials, at least for the important cults. Their titles vary from city to city. At Epidauros they are the *hiaromnamones* (the 'sacred remembrancers'), at Delos they are the *amphiktyones* and so forth. These were usually state officials, magistrates, appointed for a limited term of office, and called on to render accounts to the state when that term expired; the inscription giving the accounts of Delian Apollo in the period 377–373, referred to above, is the act of such an administrative body, complicated there by the fact that Delos was then under Athenian control, and the officials were therefore Athenian, not Delian. The term of office served by these officials varied, but in many cults a four-year cycle is discernible; normal festivals occurred every year, but every fourth year there was a particularly fine festival, called Great—the Great Panathenaia, the Great Delia, and so forth—so that officials would take up a term of office running from one great festival to the next. Through these officials the state exercised its interest in the cult and its affairs. They checked not only revenue and expenditure, but also the possessions of the cult, including the valuable offerings deposited in the temples and sanctuaries. The lists presented by them in their accounts, and recorded in inscriptions, often give a better idea of the contents of a sanctuary, particularly in terms of valuable objects, gold plate and the like, than does the surviving archaeological evidence.[12]

The financial implications of building work conform to normal Greek practice, though there must have been a distinction between the practice of sophisticated societies, which kept proper records and control, evidence for which has survived, and the less developed communities for which we have no evidence. Again, some of the fullest evidence comes from Epidauros, where regular contracts were drawn up for the work involved in the development of the sanctuary. In general terms, the priestly administrators, the *hiaromnamones*, were responsible; but the detailed arrangements and organization were the responsibility of a building commission. This commission would include the architect, and others appointed for their technical and financial abilities. They would divide the work into separate lots, and assign them in contract to different craftsmen or contractors. They would be directly responsible (to the government) for seeing that the work was properly carried out, and would be required to inspect progress. The day-to-day supervision, of course, was in the charge of the architect. Between the commissioners and the contractors carrying out the work came the guarantors. They were needed, not only in the building activity of the sanctuaries, but in any activity that involved state expenditure. They were men of social and financial standing. When a contract was made with a contractor they undertook to pay an assessed penalty should the contractor fail, or the work prove unsatisfactory. The existence of this element in the financial administration of a building programme reflects the condition of legal practice in the Greek cities, where, in general, there was no state prosecutor system for the state to lay charges, especially in what we would term civil matters, all responsibility (even for accusations of murder) being placed on individuals, either aggrieved parties or mere informers. The guarantor gave a legal assurance, as well as a financial guarantee, that the money allotted to building would be properly spent. Greek architecture owes much to these innumerable men, equally involved with the few famous architects whose names have come down to us in the creation of the splendid buildings and sanctuaries which we can still admire and appreciate today.

5   Major sanctuaries

The distinction between sanctuaries which attracted worshippers from a wide area, and those belonging to single states is imprecise. Sanctuaries normally originated to serve the communities in which they were situated, but unless they pertained to a closed cult (that is, a cult open only to those who had undergone an initiation rite) they seem to have welcomed worshippers whatever their origin. Some made no distinction between free man and slave; everyone, men and women alike, could pay their respects to the gods who controlled the fortunes of all. As a result cults might draw their patronage from a wider area. Even here it is possible to distinguish sanctuaries which, although their patronage might have come from a wide area, were still principally sanctuaries of a particular and important town—the sanctuary and cult of Athena at Athens is a good example of this—from those where the local community was small and insignificant, so that the external element was principally responsible for the support of the cult.

Three sanctuaries are of paramount importance in this respect, those at Olympia, at Delphi and on the sacred island of Delos. The sanctuary of Zeus at Olympia was in territory which in the classical period belonged to the state of Elis. More immediately, it belonged to the minor community of Pisa, apparently destroyed by the Eleans in the 470s.[1] Long before then it had attracted to its major festival—connected with the quadrennial celebration of the Olympic games—visitors from a much wider area, principally, but not exclusively, from the cities of the Peloponnese and their colonies in the West. Its importance was such that the presidency of the Olympic games was a serious matter for contention as early as the seventh (or possibly even the eighth) century BC.[2] The traditional date for the inauguration of the Olympic games, and the religious truce which enabled competitors and worshippers to come even from states which were at war with each other, was 776 BC. There is no good evidence for the continuity here of a cult from the Bronze Age. Nevertheless, the legends connected with the sanctuary and the games suggest the possibility of a Bronze Age origin. If so, it must have been situated in a slightly different site to that where the classical sanctuary developed, and its existence cannot be proved archaeologically.

In classical times there were two sanctuaries at Delphi, close to each other but physically distinct. The larger was that dedicated to Apollo, which contained the oracle; the other was dedicated to Athena. Both are on sites which were occupied and used during the Bronze Age, but only that of Athena seems possibly to have been religious in character; that under the sanctuary of Apollo, in an area of natural springs, seems rather to have been a settlement site. Again, the legends and traditions place the sacred origins of Delphi in what we would term the Bronze Age, but they also record the arrival of Apollo, and his occupation of a place which previously had been sacred to Ge (Earth) and Themis.[3] This may well be the explanation of the existence there of two distinct sanctuaries. The evidence of the offerings in the area of the Apollo sanctuary again points to the eighth century as the essential time of its development. Delphi was administered by a special council, called that of the *Amphictyones*, or those who dwell around, already implying that the sanctuary was shared by a number of neighbouring communities of central Greece, but as Delphi grew in importance so the area embraced by the Amphictyonic council increased in size. Delphi had reached considerable international importance by the seventh century BC, and the oracle was consulted on a wide range of matters by many states. By the sixth century there are signs of struggle by the major powers, such as Athens and Sparta, to control or at least to dominate the sanctuary, and even a distant potentate, King Croesus of Lydia, on the other side of the Aegean, thought it worth while wooing the oracle with lavish gifts.[4] Thus the international role of the sanctuary was clearly recognized by this time, and its fortunes developed accordingly. Dedications made there show that it was well regarded by the mainland Greeks, by those of the West (though perhaps less so than Olympia), by the Greeks of north Africa and the Aegean area.

For the Aegean Greeks, however, it is clear that the island of Delos was the principal sanctuary of Apollo. The island is small, rocky and naturally waterless. It could never, of its own resources, have been a place of population, and since its importance cannot be explained by normal economic factors, it seems reasonable to suppose that there, too, it was the religious factor which made the place significant, both in the classical period and the preceding late Bronze Age. Delos is too small to have stood alone; and again, this seems to be a sanctuary dominated by communities standing outside the immediate locality. It appears to have developed as a place of religious significance to the populations of the neighbouring larger islands, Tenos, Paros and, above all in the archaic age, Naxos. By the sixth century Athens was taking a lively interest in the fortunes of the island and its sanctuary. In the fifth century, and for long periods afterwards, though with occasional interludes, she controlled it. The Delian festival was essentially one for maritime communities. Participating cities sent official delegations in state warships, Athens possessing two special triremes, the *Salaminia* and the *Paralos*, for such purposes. It is interesting that the same ritual, transformed into a festival of the Christian church, is still observed on the feast of the Assumption on neighbouring Tenos, when a warship of the Greek navy is despatched from Piraeus by the government.

Olympia

Olympia is situated in the valley of the river Alpheios, which flows westwards from the central Peloponnese.[5] Further inland the river has carved its way through limestone gorges, and the present main road, which runs approximately in the same direction, has to leave the line of river, twisting and climbing in series of hairpin bends through the hills and tributary valleys. It is not, therefore, a place which can be said to have easy communications with the classical centres on the other side of the Peloponnese. By the time it reaches the vicinity of Olympia the river has opened into a broader valley: the sanctuary itself is on flatter ground, immediately to the south of a low conical hill called the hill of Kronos (who in the Greek mythology was the father of Zeus), and at the confluence of the last principal tributary river to the Alpheios, the Kladeos. The valley is well watered and pleasant; the neighbouring hills and, indeed, the sanctuary itself, are clothed in pine-trees (plate 7). The severity of mountain Greece is here relaxed.

The sanctuary was known as the *Altis*: according to Pausanias this is the local dialect form of the word meaning 'grove'. When the area can first be recognized it is roughly rectangular in shape, about 650 by 520 feet (200 by 160 metres) (fig. 9). It was eventually defined, on the sides that were not closed by buildings, by a boundary wall; but this does not seem to have been built before the end of the fourth century BC. Before this, it is unlikely that there was any visible boundary, but a distinction must somehow have been recognized between the areas within and outside the sanctuary. It is most unlikely that the fourth-century boundary in any way restricted the sacred area; so that even with buildings which are older than the wall, it is possible to distinguish between those that are inside and those that are outside the sanctuary.

Today the sanctuary is approached by a modern road from the north-west; this was not the principal ancient approach, and must be disregarded in any assessment of the ancient layout and arrangement of the sanctuary. The ancient road crossed the Kladeos further to the south, and passed first outside the southern limits of the sanctuary. The main road continued beyond, but a 'sacred way' led to the north, entering the sanctuary at its south-eastern corner, near the point later marked by a Roman gateway (in the form of a triumphal arch) built in connection with the visit of Nero in AD 66.

The ritual centre of the sanctuary was the altar of Zeus, at which the sacrifices were made. Unusually, this was not a built structure, but a simple heap made from the ashes of the sacrificial fires. That this was the original focus of the cult there can be no doubt, and we imagine the first worshippers finding—and developing—merely this ash-altar in a clearing of the sacred grove. To judge from the datable objects found in the sanctuary, which indicate that offerings were being made, this dates back to the tenth century BC. The buildings in the sanctuary belong to subsequent periods of development, and reflect its growing importance, centring on the Olympic games. For these a place of athletic contest and an area for the chariot races had to be set aside. The stadium lies to the north-east of the sanctuary, entered through a vaulted passage (plate 8). The stadium now visible has been partly restored after excavation, and belongs to the fourth century BC. The remains of a fifth-century predecessor were also found, underlying it but beginning further to the west, that is, within the area demarcated in the fourth century as belonging to the sanctuary in the strict sense, though the greater part extended beyond. This was not, of course, the earliest; there are stones which appear to belong to a sixth-century stadium. Whether there was any formal stadium before this date is problematical; it was the sixth century which saw the beginning of athletic contests in other sanctuaries. But it was firmly believed that the first Olympic truce (necessary for competitors to travel to the games) was declared in 776 BC and there is no valid reason for not accepting this as, at least, a strong probability. If so the next stage in the development of Olympia must have been the institution of the games; but at first we must suppose, as with the cult of Zeus, that this took place in natural surroundings without any buildings or structures to accommodate it. It is interesting to compare the sanctuary of Poseidon at Isthmia, scene of the Isthmian games, where the original stadium was situated close to the temple, and consisted of a running track without special arrangements for the spectators; this was later moved further from the sanctuary in the strict sense, and given the seating for spectators. At Olympia, in this area outside the strict sanctuary there was also the place where the chariot races were held, the most prestigious of the athletic events in the Olympic games.

During the remainder of the archaic period, down to the time of the Persian wars at the beginning of the fifth century BC, there were three principal developments, the temple of Hera, the so-called 'treasuries', and the *bouleuterion*, or council house.

The temple of Hera lies in the north-west corner of the sanctuary, immediately below the lower slopes of the hill of Kronos (plate 9). At present one can still see the two-stepped platform on which it stood, with the stone footing of its walls, and three of its stone columns, re-erected after the excavations. The temple is essentially the work of the early sixth century BC, though it is clear from the bewildering differences in the proportions of the columns and the shapes of the capitals surmounting them that it originally was built with wooden columns, which were replaced, gradually, over a long period of time, but beginning not long after the original construction. The building history of the temple has been much disputed. Dörpfeld, the great German scholar, believed that the original temple was constructed about 1000 BC. These theories have been modified as a result of further archaeological investigation, and a more recent view is that there was an older temple of the seventh century which was replaced (or rather reconstructed) at the beginning of the sixth. Even this theory is now believed to be too complicated, and a reinvestigation of the structures on the south side has led to the idea that the sixth-century temple is in fact the first. The possibility nevertheless remains that simpler, earlier structures did exist; the area of the temple was certainly a place of cult before the construction of the surviving temple.

The temple itself was possibly old-fashioned even when it was first constructed. There is no good building stone in the vicinity of Olympia, and the first stone temples had been built already in other sanctuaries; this explains why the replacement of the wooden columns began so shortly after the original construction. Its area is 61 feet 6 inches by 164 feet 1 inch (18.76 by 50.0 metres) when measured at the top step (*stylobate*). There are six columns across the façades and sixteen along the flanks, the corner column being counted twice; thus it is long and narrow by the standards of the fifth century, but conforms with the proportions usually found in the earlier temples of the sixth century. The walls were of mud brick over a carefully worked stone footing. The roof was formed from terracotta tiles supported, it would seem, completely by timber—timber rafters and beams, timber entablature over originally timber columns, and presumably a timber sole-plate on the wall. In appearance, the temple must have been rather unimpressive, at least in later times, to eyes more accustomed to the proportions of the fifth century. The columns were of no great height—17 feet 1½ inches (5.21 metres)—and the roof would probably have appeared heavy, giving the temple a squatness and massiveness foreign to later taste. It was, in all probability, rather plain. No decorated metopes, no pedimental sculptures have survived, and the principal embellishment appears to have been large discs (*acroteria*) over the gables, made of terracotta and decorated in a strictly geometric pattern.

Despite its quaintness the temple survived, probably until the end of the third century AD, overshadowed by its greater and more impressive neighbour, the fifth-century temple of Zeus, but obviously venerated as an ancient monument which could not be replaced arbitrarily by a more up-to-date structure. It would seem that, despite the name usually bestowed on the temple, it contained a statue of Zeus as well as of his consort, Hera; so in a sense the later temple is a replacement. Even so, the old temple was not only allowed to remain but kept under repair, the wooden columns being replaced as necessary.

The treasuries stood on a low terrace, which was raised above the general level of the sanctuary along its northern end and placed between the temple and the approach to the stadium (plate 10). They consist essentially of small temple-like buildings, with a porch and an inner room of similar width behind. Most (but not all) have porches consisting of two Doric columns between the forward continuations of the side walls. These were buildings dedicated as gifts to the god by individual Greek cities, often to commemorate a military victory (normally at the expense of another city). All but three belong to the sixth century BC. The three oldest were dedicated by Greek colonies in the west, two from Italy (Sybaris and Metapontum), one from Sicily (Gela). The other sixth-century examples were built by Epidauros, Cyrene, Selinus and Megara. The row was thus almost completed by the end of the sixth century; of the later treasuries that of Byzantium was placed in an apparently vacant space between that of Epidauros and that of Sybaris; the other two (Sikyon and Syracuse) were placed at the beginning of the line. One other, of the sixth century, the seventh in the sequence from east to west, is of unknown dedication.

Several interesting points emerge from a study of these buildings (quite apart from their intrinsic architectural qualities). They are dedicated mostly by Dorian Greek communities, emphasizing the importance of Olympia at a relatively early stage in its history to this particular group of Greeks. It is also noticeable that the majority (and certainly the earliest) were given by cities which were geographically remote from Olympia, being situated overseas. Perhaps the feeling that the city should have, as it were, a permanent foothold in the sanctuary was important. Finally, this is the only group of buildings which was essentially complete by the time of the Persian invasions—indeed, the north side of the sanctuary, including the temple of Hera, was little altered in later times. It is difficult to see why the custom of building treasuries died out; a possible explanation is the development of sculpture, and of the custom of dedicating statuary and other outdoor monuments which is typical of the fifth century BC and later.

The early buildings round the sanctuary are completed by the two parts of the *bouleuterion* or council house. This comprises two long apsidal buildings facing east with porches of three columns. The northern building is the earlier, and dates perhaps to the middle of the sixth century; the southern belongs to the end of the century. Though they were subsequently joined by a central room and a colonnade they were originally distinct. Yet their similarity of form makes it likely that they had the same function, that they housed two groups performing similar administrative duties. How the two groups were distinguished is purely a matter of speculation; it has been suggested that one represented the controlling city-state of Elis, the other the local

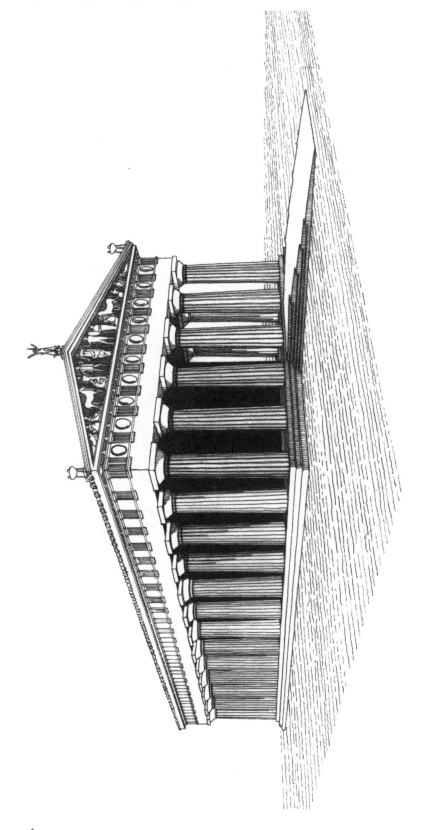

10 Olympia: the temple of Zeus, perspective reconstruction

community of Pisa. When the boundary wall to the sanctuary was constructed, this building was left outside. So whatever its function, it was regarded as an ancillary building, connected with the sanctuary and its observances, but one which did not have to stand in the most strictly sacred area.

Olympia was not affected by the Persian invasions of 490 and 480, unlike Delos (which the Persians occupied and subsequently was used as a base for the Greek fleet) or Delphi (which sided with the Persians in anticipation of what seemed their inevitable victory). The states of the Peloponnese, for whom Olympia was the most important sanctuary, formed under the leadership of Sparta the core of Greek resistance to the Persians; and it would be natural to expect to find there tangible evidence of monuments constructed to commemorate the Greek victory.

The first and major addition to the sanctuary after the Persian wars was the temple of Zeus (plate 11 and fig. 10). According to Pausanias (who, it would seem, reported what he learnt at Olympia itself in the second century AD), it was built by the city of Elis from the spoils they took when they captured Pisa; the architect was a local man called Libon.[7] Elis destroyed Pisa in 471; the temple is known to have been structurally complete by 458 at the very latest, when monuments were placed on the gable end by the Spartans to commemorate their defeat of the Athenians and their allies at the battle of Tanagra.[8] At the time it was built it would seem to have been the largest temple in mainland Greece, measuring 90 feet 10 inches by 210 feet $4\frac{1}{2}$ inches (27.68 by 64.12 metres). The Athenians at the end of the sixth century had begun a larger temple in their own city, also dedicated to Zeus, but this had hardly proceeded beyond foundation level; it was not until the 430s that they completed the Parthenon, whose original dimensions were altered so that the finished temple just exceeds that at Olympia in size. The sculptural decoration in the pediment at the east end of the temple at Olympia (that is, of course, the front of the temple) has as its theme the chariot race between Pelops and Oinomaos, the legendary first race at Olympia; this is entirely relevant to the local significance of the temple. At the west end, however, the sculpture depicts the struggle at the wedding of Peirithoos when the centaurs, who had been invited, got drunk and tried to rape the women. Peirithoos was king of the Lapiths, and his kingdom was in Thessaly, far away from Olympia; and he was helped in the struggle by Theseus, King of Athens, who was also his guest. Pausanias attempts to relate this to the cult of Zeus at Olympia: Peirithoos was a son of Zeus, and Theseus the great-grandson of Pelops; this explanation, however, seems a little strained, and since the struggle between centaurs and Lapiths comes to be used frequently in Greek art to symbolize the struggle between the Persian barbarians and the Greeks, the possibility of a wider significance at Olympia should be considered. Thus it might be that the temple is a thank offering for the victory of the Greeks over the Persians, constructed in the sanctuary which was particularly favoured by the Peloponnesian leader of the anti-Persian alliance.

The temple is in the Doric order, with six massive columns (far sturdier than those of the Parthenon) across the façade and thirteen along the flanks. The entablature is equally weighty and severely plain. The stone from which it is constructed, the local marine conglomerate, full of shells, is very coarse and cannot take a fine finish. It was totally unsuitable for sculpture, and in the structural parts of temple had to be coated with a fine hard white stucco. The sculptural decoration was executed in imported island marble; apart from the pediment sculptures, the metopes over the inner columns of the front and rear porches were carved; they depict the labours of Herakles, the legendary ancestor of the two Spartan royal families, perhaps another indication of Sparta's interest in the construction of the temple as an offering for the Spartan-led victory over the Persian invader. The temple was famous for its cult statue, a colossal image of Zeus seated on a throne, made by the Athenian Pheidias in gold and ivory, a rival to the same artist's statue of Athena in the Parthenon. This was made, it would seem, after Pheidias was expelled from Athens in the 430s and was not part of the original plan for the temple; indeed, it was out of scale with the temple (despite the fact that the building was only slightly smaller than the Parthenon) and it was remarked that if Zeus had ever got up from his throne, he would have taken the roof with him. The statue was made in a separate building just outside the western boundary of the sanctuary, the workshop of Pheidias—a remarkably solid building, which was eventually converted into a church. Other minor buildings of the fifth century were constructed in the same area; they do not affect the appearance of the sanctuary.

It is difficult to visualize the appearance of the sanctuary in the fifth century from the surviving remains of the temple. This stood until the sixth century AD, repaired on occasions after damage caused by earthquake. Abandoned then and roofless it was finally overthrown by yet another earthquake. Only the platform survives, surrounded by the fallen columns whose poor stone has often disintegrated badly. The sculptures, thrown and shattered when the temple fell, are now in the nearby museum. When it was intact, coated with white stucco, with the usual coloured decoration of the Doric order and its splendid pediment sculptures, the temple would have dominated the sanctuary by size and the magnificence of its display. In the northeast corner, against the slope of the hill, the old temple of Hera would have seemed insignificant, not because it was very much smaller than the new temple, but because it was lower and its forms less impressive. All later building must stand in relationship to the fifth-century temple.

By the end of the fifth century the sanctuary had acquired a considerable number of non-architectural monuments, principally sculpture. It had always been the practice to make dedicatory offerings to the gods and many of these, bronze figurines and other objects, have been found at Olympia dating back to the seventh and eighth centuries BC. Towards the end of the seventh century Greece adopted from Egyptian sources the art of monumental sculpture; and though some of these statues were placed in the various buildings, they were obviously more often suited to stand outside. The materials used were terracotta, marble or limestone, and bronze (exceptionally, cult-statues such as that of Zeus were made of gold plates and ivory fixed to a wooden core; such statues had perforce to be indoors, and, despite the sanctity of the area in which they stood, under lock and key). Olympia did not differ in this respect from other sanctuaries, and though the statues have gone (for the few that survived to be discovered by the excavators are too precious to be left outside, and have been moved to the two Olympia museums), the bases on which they stood generally survive, often with sufficient marks on them to indicate the type, size and pose of the statue, or statue group they carried.

Pausanias gives an account of the principal sculptures; there is not room here to describe them all. Particularly important were the series called *Zanes*, which stood in a row in front of the treasuries, lining the route from the temple of Hera to the Stadium, where sixteen bases for them have been found. Though none of the statues survives, the bases (and their name, which is the plural of the Eleian dialect form of Zeus) suggest that they were nude bronzes depicting Zeus striding forward and hurling his thunderbolt. These were not dedications; they were paid for (so Pausanias tells us) from fines exacted from athletes who dishonoured the games. The positioning of them was obviously deliberate and appropriate. The earliest of them—six in number—were set up in 388 BC.

By the end of the fourth century the sanctuary was complete. It now contained an additional small temple, in the Doric order, dedicated to the mother-goddess and placed between the Heraion and the terrace of the treasuries. The eastern side was marked by an extensive stoa, known as the Echo Colonnade, which formed a boundary to the sanctuary on that side, closing it off from the stadium except for the entrance passage by the treasuries and the Zanes. In the north-west corner is a building called the *prytaneion*, which had undergone several periods of reconstruction; these were confused in the nineteenth-century excavations. The building has recently been elucidated; its main function was to act as a formal dining-room.[9]

Another important structure was the monument put up by Philip II of Macedon near the temple of Hera, commemorating his victory over Athens and Thebes at Chaironeia in 338 BC. It is a circular structure, or *tholos*, with a conical roof and surrounded by an outer colonnade of Ionic columns in the particular variant form used in Peloponnesian architecture, having only twenty flutes to the columns as in the Doric order and with capitals having volutes on all four sides, not merely front and back. The same form was subsequently used to decorate a tomb in Macedon, by the royal palace at Vergina; and Philip's monument at Olympia in a sense also recalls his tragic assassination, only two years after his great victory. It contained gold and ivory statues of himself, his wife, Olympias, his mother and father, Eurydike and Amyntas, and his son, Alexander the Great.

The remaining development, chiefly of the Hellenistic age, is concentrated on the area outside the sanctuary enclosure, in the secondary region where ancillary structures were located. They include another stoa, the south stoa, beyond the *bouleuterion*, while on the west side various structures were put up on either side of Pheidias' workshop; to the north a courtyard building with a formal entrance for athletic exercise (the *palaistra*—plate 12) and a much larger court, the gymnasium. To the south a complicated courtyard building, the gift of one Leonidas (not, of course, the fifth-century Spartan king of that name, who died at Thermopylae in 480 BC), served to provide sleeping accommodation for distinguished guests. All these buildings reflect the Hellenistic desire to improve the amenities in the sanctuaries for the human visitors and worshippers, rather than the cult of the gods. They were lavishly constructed, with stone colonnades, and though not laid out to any organized plan, the buildings' presence round the sanctuary is of architectural importance to it, emphasizing to an increasing extent its closed-in nature.

Olympia is one of the very few sanctuaries in mainland Greece which continued to be embellished in Roman times. The 'Triumphal Arch' of Nero has already been mentioned. There is also a series of rooms and courtyards known as the 'House of

Nero' in the south-east parts outside the sanctuary which are difficult to elucidate. The most terrific Roman monument, however, was the semi-domed *Nymphaeum* or grandiose fountain house built on the north side of the sanctuary under the hill of Kronos and at the west end of the terrace of the treasuries by the millionaire landowner and philanthropist of the second century AD, Herodes Atticus. This building is in an alien style, and quite out of proportion to its surroundings. It creates an impression of brash vitality which is quite artificial; by this time the sanctuaries were entering their twilight slumber, having long lost their religious significance and meaning in the much changed society of Roman times.

Delphi

The sanctuary of Apollo at Delphi is situated on the southern slopes of Mount Parnassus, on a narrow natural terrace overlooking a deep river valley, and with distant views of the gulf of Corinth (fig. 11).[10] It is a wild spot, bare and rocky, in marked contrast with the apparently unbroken extent of olive trees in the valley and plain below. In antiquity there was a small town or village at Delphi itself, but this was unimportant. The district in which Delphi was situated was Phocis, a relatively backward part of Greece which was late to develop urban centres. The Phocians were not responsible for the development of the sanctuary, or for the international influence of Delphian Apollo.

How and why the sanctuary developed this importance is a mystery. Apollo is almost certainly an intruder (there was a tradition that he usurped the sanctuary) and it is unlikely that he arrived before the end of the Bronze Age; if so, his arrival is probably to be connected with the movements of Greek peoples in that confused period. On another terrace, a little below that on which Apollo's sanctuary was situated, was a separate sanctuary of Athena; here there have been found the usual terracottas and other objects which may be held to indicate that this was a place of cult in the late Bronze Age, so that it would seem that Apollo established himself by the side of an existing cult. Even so, there is the inevitable lack of archaeological evidence for continuity of cult through the dark ages.

The influence of Apollo derived from the fact that his shrine was oracular.[11] By the sixth century it was clearly the principal oracular shrine in Greece, and though it did not have a monopoly, its reliability and reputation was such that Delphian Apollo's advice was sought in preference to that of other gods. The nature of oracular responses is an indication of the part they played in the life of the Greek states, and the reason for their importance. The oracle did not give general responses about the future (an area where, to anyone judging matters from the point of view of modern scepticism rather than ancient religious belief, it is obvious that the chances of successful prediction were minimal, and where therefore there was no likelihood of a reputation being developed). Instead, it gave specific answers to specific problems. Further, consultation of the oracle was as likely to be made on behalf of the state as the individual—reflecting the importance of the community's needs, rather than

11 *Opposite*, Delphi: plan of the sanctuary of Apollo (after *Fouilles de Delphes*)

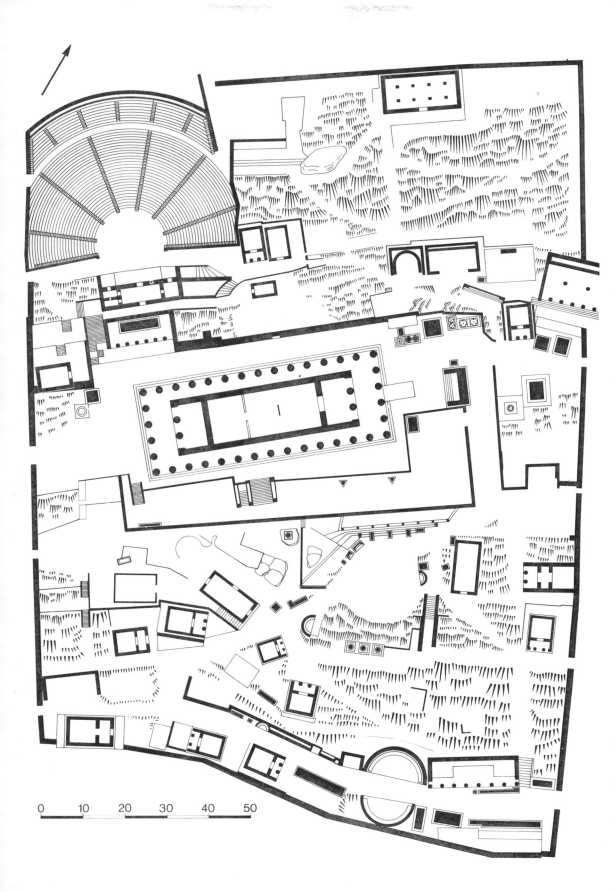

0   10   20   30   40   50

those of individual beliefs, in the practice of ancient Greek religion. There can be no doubt that the oracle fostered this development. In particular, it acted as a sort of clearing house for the development of the Greek world in the archaic period, receiving advice and information from one city which consulted it, passing it on where appropriate to others. As its influence grew, so Greek cities with ambitions felt the need to influence or even control the oracle, and it is possible to detect changes in the political implications of its responses. It is easy to see why, in these circumstances and despite its geographical remoteness, it became a sanctuary of universal importance.

The oracular responses were made by a priestess, the Pythia, from an inner room in the temple. The method of response was, it seems, connected with a sacred spring; the priestess went into a trance, and her ravings were interpreted, being given to the person consulting her in the form of regular dactylic poetry. The consulting person for his part had to perform a set ritual before the consultation took place, including a purification. The architectural setting for this was the temple, which included in its plan the necessary inner room for the priestess, which had access to a space below the floor level, connected no doubt with the trances. Here we have a sanctuary where the temple functioned as more than the normal house of the god and place of offering. The modifications to its arrangement to make the oracular usage possible were not that considerable, and outwardly it formed a conventional Doric peripteral temple (plate 13). There is an altar in front of it, to the east. The terrace on which the sanctuary and the temple stand lies underneath steep cliffs. It is in an area subject to earth tremors, which from time to time had the disastrous consequence of loosening large boulders from the cliff tops, to crash destructively on the sanctuary below. On several occasions the temple was destroyed or badly damaged, and there was therefore a succession of structures on the site. The early building history of the temple has not been elucidated (Greek legend maintained a fanciful knowledge of the earliest temples) but in view of the need for a building to accommodate the oracle, we must suppose a very early original building. It reached its definitive form in the sixth century BC, though that building was destroyed in the fourth century; at that time, however, the reconstruction seems to have followed faithfully the lines of the sixth-century building. It measures 71 feet 1½ inches by 190 feet 10½ inches (21.68 by 58.18 metres).

The sixth-century temple involved fairly massive reorganization of the area in which it stood. The temple itself was presumably enlarged at this time (perhaps to accommodate for the first time a surrounding colonnade) and its platform required artificial support. A great terrace wall, with blocks of irregular shape and size but with the curved lines used particularly in the second part of the sixth century, runs across the middle of the sanctuary (plate 14). The platform held not only the temple, but the area in front of it and its altar. The temple, in both the sixth- and fourth-century versions, was essentially a limestone structure, built of local stone. Marble quarries were remote, and though marble could be shipped cheaply to the harbour on the Gulf of Corinth below the sanctuary, to transport large blocks uphill to the sanctuary would have been a costly business. Nevertheless marble was used in the sixth-century building, for the façade and the pedimental sculpture. The story recorded was that the Athenian aristocrat and politician Kleisthenes, then being in exile because Athens was under the unconstitutional control of Hippias the tyrant, undertook the contract for the rebuilding of the temple.[12] This specified the use of local limestone; Kleisthenes built partly in marble, meeting the additional expense out of his own pocket, in a successful attempt to win the support of the oracle for the overthrow of Hippias. The story has been doubted, for the style of the temple and its sculpture suggests an earlier date than the years just before 510, when Hippias was finally driven out; but the attempt to win the support of Delphi could well antedate the overthrow of the tyrant by several years, and it is likely that Kleisthenes was then in full possession of his landed property in Attica and so able to afford the additional expense.

The remainder of the sanctuary both below and above the temple platform slopes steeply, and it is hardly surprising that no regular or coherent plan was attainable. The unifying principle was the need to provide a reasonable line of access, passable by the solemn procession and sacrificial animals, from the lowest point in the sanctuary up to the area of the temple and altar. The sanctuary itself was marked by a precinct wall, giving an approximately rectangular area. The lowest point is at the south-east corner, and it is here that the approach road, the sacred way enters. The road itself was paved in Roman times, and its line inside the sanctuary (and the immediate approach outside) is clear. There was no formal gateway. From the start, the sacred way rises steadily, flanked by commemorative monuments, those even of enemies to one another placed almost side by side. As it nears (but does not in fact reach) the western perimeter, the road turns sharply and runs upwards still but towards the east. At the turn it passes in front of a small Doric building, the treasury of the Athenians built at about the turn of the sixth and fifth centuries as an offering to Apollo in gratitude for victory (which victory depends on the precise date of the building, which in its turn depends on the subjective evaluation of its architectural forms and the carving of its metopes; either the double victory over Chalcis and Thebes in 506, or, more likely, the battle of Marathon and the resounding defeat of the Persians in 490).[13]

The building as it now stands is reconstructed, mostly from the original material which was discovered by the French excavators of Delphi, scattered over the hillside below. It is interesting that Athens was able to achieve such a dominant position for its treasury; since it was built after the downfall of the tyranny, and at a time when Kleisthenes was either in control of Athens himself or had but recently died, this might bear out the stories of the influence which he had secured there. The present dominance of the Athenian treasury is enhanced by its relative completeness; in the sixth and fifth centuries many others were built, of which only the foundations survive in situ. Of these, only reconstructions on paper are possible. The Athenian treasury would have been much more crowded in by those other treasuries in antiquity; nevertheless, its position, so close to the turn in the sacred way, is an excellent one.

Few other monuments at Delphi, though important in themselves, are particularly significant in the arrangement of the sanctuary; their position is determined by factors other than religious usage or the desire for an attractive and regular plan. The main feature is obviously the sacred way, particularly for monuments which are intended to be visual demonstrations of their donor's piety, since it was preferable for these to be placed where people were in fact most likely to notice them. There were several monuments in what one would suppose to have been the prime location, by the temple itself. Of these the most famous was the monument commemorating the victory of the united Greeks over the Persians at the battle of Plataea; a bronze tripod and snake, the names of the cities forming the Greek alliance being inscribed on the body of the snake. At Delphi only the foundation and the base remain; but the snake survives in Istanbul, where it was taken in the early fourth century AD to be an adornment of Constantine's new city, at the time when Delphi itself was moribund. Other monuments in this area include several commemorative pillars or columns, including a late fifth-century example by the Syracusans to mark their fatal destruction of the Athenian expedition against them in 412, and some interesting Hellenistic monuments (including a double column surmounted by a fragmentary entablature) put up by private individuals (plate 15).

Above the sanctuary were several buildings and a spring. The buildings included one called the 'club' (*lesche*) of the Cnidians, which once contained famous panel paintings by the artist Polygnotos. The building is badly damaged, and of course nothing of the paintings survives. What precisely was its function is difficult to say. It was presumably of itself an offering to Apollo. It may have been used by worshippers from the east Greek city of Cnidos (mindful of their mainland, Dorian ancestry) as a gathering place, perhaps for ritual meals at the time of sacrifice. Beyond this and forming the north-west part of the precinct is the theatre (plate 16). By the side of the Lesche and just below the theatre was a monument commemorating Alexander the Great, with sculptures depicting the king engaged in a lion hunt, a strange intrusion of the oriental symbolism of royal prestige into a Greek sanctuary. The theatre itself is well preserved, as far as its stone seating is concerned. The missing stage building may have obscured part of the view from the lower seats over the rest of the sanctuary, but otherwise it affords an excellent outlook. At the same time, it must be admitted that a theatre-type of structure anywhere at Delphi could hardly fail to give an excellent view, and the extent to which this was deliberately planned may be doubted.

The separate sanctuary of Athena is situated on a lower terrace, a little to the east of Apollo's (plate 17). This terrace is narrow, and the buildings on it inevitably strung out along it. The temple is at the end furthest from the sanctuary of Apollo. Here again there is evidence of constant rebuilding, for this terrace, like that of Apollo, is vulnerable to boulders dislodged from the cliffs above it. There is an early stone temple with slender columns of the late seventh century BC, which was twice rebuilt or replaced in the sixth and fourth centuries. By the temple stands a circular Doric building, partly reconstructed, and given the generic name applied in antiquity to circular buildings in Greek sanctuaries, the tholos (plate 18). It is a slightly earlier example (though still of the fourth century BC) of a type of building to be found also in the sanctuary of Asklepios at Epidauros. Its function as a building is uncertain. Circular structures of this sort are not at all common in Greek sanctuaries, and it is noticeable that there are problems of interpretation whenever a building of unusual design or appearance occurs. The tholos is not a temple in circular form, though architecturally it could be described in this way. That it was an important part of the sanctuary seems clear enough; it is a building of architectural merit on which considerable expense has been lavished (in this respect also it is similar to the tholos at Epidauros); moreover, it is a replacement for a sixth-century predecessor. Pausanias' description of the sanctuary ignores it completely; it may have been in ruins by his time. Apart from the temples and the tholos this sanctuary also had treasuries; that built by Massalia (Marseilles) has the unusual leaf-capital to its columns which apparently originates in the north-west parts of what is now Turkey (Phocaea, the mother-city of Massalia, is situated in this region).

There are various other buildings outside the sanctuaries, some of them belonging to the town or village rather than serving a specifically religious purpose. Crucially important is the spring of Kastalia, an abundant source of cool water which issues from a cleft in the cliffs more or less midway between the two sanctuaries. This was improved by cutting away the rock, and constructing a fountain house in front of it. It supplied water to the worshippers, for purification before entering the sanctuary as well as for normal use, and to the town. Below the spring and fed from it was a gymnasium, with a circular pool for bathing. There are other buildings close to the sanctuary of Apollo (which itself lay 'above' the town). These include a portico built by the Pergamene King Attalos, which no doubt would have been constructed in the sanctuary itself if there had been room available. Instead, it had to breach the precinct wall, extending for some distance beyond it to the east. It is a typical Pergamene structure using terrace substructures to secure a sufficient platform on a sloping site, and making considerable use of arches and vaulting in its structure. The walls appear to have been fitted out to receive wooden panels which carried paintings, but nothing of these has survived. On the other side of the sanctuary, beyond the theatre, is the stadium for the athletic contests of the Pythian games; its distance from the sanctuary is probably dictated by the difficulty in finding a sufficiently extensive flat area for its creation. On the outer side its seats were supported on an artificial terrace bank. Other structures outside the sanctuary include a substantial tomb monument, with an underground, vaulted burial chamber beneath a courtyard building which could be used to accommodate some form of commemorative ritual. This tomb is of Hellenistic date, at a time when private, but wealthy, individuals were leaving money for the establishment of a private commemorative cult after their death. There is a similar, better preserved tomb at Kalydon in Aetolia, near the sanctuary of Artemis; Delphi belonged to the Aetolian league at the time the tomb was constructed there.[14]

Viewed from the other side of the valley which lies below Delphi, the sanctuary appears insignificant, the puny columns of the temple being difficult to make out against the overpowering backcloth of cliff. Any human endeavour in such a context is bound to be puny, compared with the tremendous architecture of nature; and anything which was built there had to take its natural setting into account. The restrictions this imposed were considerable. The sites of both sanctuaries, of Apollo and Athena, are severely limited, that of Apollo by the steepness of the slope and the irregularity of the surface enclosed, that of Athena by the narrowness of the terrace, and its general inaccessibility, except at either end. In both, buildings have to be adapted to the natural difficulties, and placed where there was a suitable space. Only the most important building, the temple-oracle of Apollo himself, could command the resources needed to alter the geography of the site to suit the larger scale of building (that is, before the Pergamene kings could do the same thing, from the wealth of their kingdom, for the less significant stoa that they built). The terrace built for the sixth-century temple is a massive work (though earlier comparable terraces had been built elsewhere—for example, at the sanctuary of Hera in the Argolid). But this terrace makes no attempt to alter the total layout or geography of the sanctuary; it creates merely an enlarged platform for an enlarged temple, in the position within the sanctuary where the temple had already stood. In architectural principle and design this is no different from the smaller footings created as individual platforms for other buildings, such as the treasury of the Athenians, or the Lesche of the Cnidians. It has no part in any thorough reorganization of the sanctuary.

So the sanctuary remained, throughout its existence, unplanned and unorganized, its arrangements dictated entirely by the site, and the winding, gradual approach from the entrance to the temple, and out, above, to the fountain Kassotis, the theatre and the stadium. Even if the funds had been available for the thorough reorganization of the site, an orderly arrangement of its monuments would have seemed incongruous against the overpowering background. Instead, the visitor to the sanctuary would have felt enclosed as much by the monuments as the cliffs behind the sanctuary, and so, since they were nearer to him, more aware of them. A more regular plan would have opened up the sanctuary, made the distant view more noticeable, and so distracted from the view of the monuments. Clearly, the religious purpose of the sanctuary is more directly served by the confused, natural arrangement than by a conscious plan.

The path of the sacred way must have created different stages of awareness within the sanctuary. Since it is in such a ruined state, it is impossible to visualize within the sanctuary in its present form exactly what was visible and what was not. At the entrance to the precinct the temple is now clearly visible. It would have been less so with monuments and treasuries intervening, but, being itself in a more complete state, there must have been enough openings and spaces through which part at least would have been seen. At this point, the visitor would have been aware of the presence of the temple, brooding over the sanctuary, as it were, but he would not yet have been able to comprehend it fully as a building. At the first turn in the sacred way it would have been more obvious, standing clear of the lower buildings, such as the stoa of the Athenians. At this stage it would have been comprehensible as a building; the viewer would have had a real sense of its size, its proportions, and the detailing of its columns. Yet it was not the complete revelation; that remained until the worshipper had ascended the second stage of the sacred way, and turned into the flat area by the altar, in front of the temple. There he would have seen not only the architecture, but the sculptural decoration, above all the figures in the pediment, which explains the significance of the temple. This was the heart of the matter; it was this which counted in Greek sanctuaries, not merely the architectural impressiveness. The temples and the other structures and offerings were not cold, dead monuments, or mere tourist attractions.

During the Roman period, the sanctuary gradually faded away. No additional monuments of any importance were added. It is difficult to give the exact moment of its death. This is usually associated with the famous last response of the oracle, given to the Roman emperor Julian in the 360s: 'Say to the King, the well-wrought hall has fallen to the ground. Phoibos no longer has his hut, nor prophetic laurel, nor the babbling spring. The babbling water is quenched.'[15] Julian had attempted, after the conversion of the empire to Christianity, a revival of paganism. The response of the oracle (made by a priest, not the Pythia) bears all the signs of a special, artificial revival for the occasion. The real death had come long before.

Delos

The sacred island of Delos lies in the central Aegean, among the Cyclades. It is small, about three miles in total length, narrow and infertile. It has no rivers, no perpetual springs, and is not a place which could from its own resources ever have attracted a substantial population. Even the neighbouring islands of Rheneia and Mykonos were not important places in antiquity. Yet Delos became one of the principal sanctuaries of the Greek world, the cult of Apollo being fostered not only by the people of the Cycladic islands but also by the Athenians, and even, at one juncture in its history and admittedly for political rather than religious reasons, by the king of Persia. The whole island was, in theory, sacred and under the normal taboos which applied within the boundaries of sanctuaries. People were not allowed to die or be buried there, and women were not allowed to give birth; if either event seemed likely to occur, the person concerned was hastily evacuated to nearby Rheneia. These taboos were not always observed; there was a community on Delos, and even places of burial, though the island was from time to time 'purified' by the removal of the burials. The development of the island is primarily religious, and there can be no doubt that if it had not been of religious importance, it would have been completely neglected and uninhabited, used perhaps as other uninhabited Aegean islands are, mainly as pasturage for sheep and goats.

It is not possible to see why the island developed its religious importance. There is strong evidence for a cult place in the late Bronze Age, and since there appears to have been no major disruption of population in the Cyclades at the end of the late Bronze Age, the existence of a continuous cult is here a virtual certainty; but this does not do more than put back the problem of its origin to remoter and therefore even more mysterious times.[16] Since we cannot see into the minds of the prehistoric peoples in the Aegean area, we cannot interpret the reasons for their action. The original divinity of Delos would seem to have been female; and in the form of the Greek (or rather Hellenized) goddess Artemis she was still worshipped there in classical times. But by the classical period the chief deity of Delos was, of course, the god Apollo; the legend was that he and Artemis (who then became his sister) were born there to their mother Leto who, driven out from other places, had found refuge in what was then a 'floating island'. As a mark of gratitude the island was then fixed in its permanent position. Various places on the island were connected with the myth, and helped to create the sacred character of the entire area.

Apart from this generally sacred character of the island, the sanctuary in the stricter sense was developed gradually, on the lower land facing towards Rheneia (fig. 12).

12 *Overleaf*, Delos: plan of the sanctuary area (after *Exploration archéologique de Délos*)

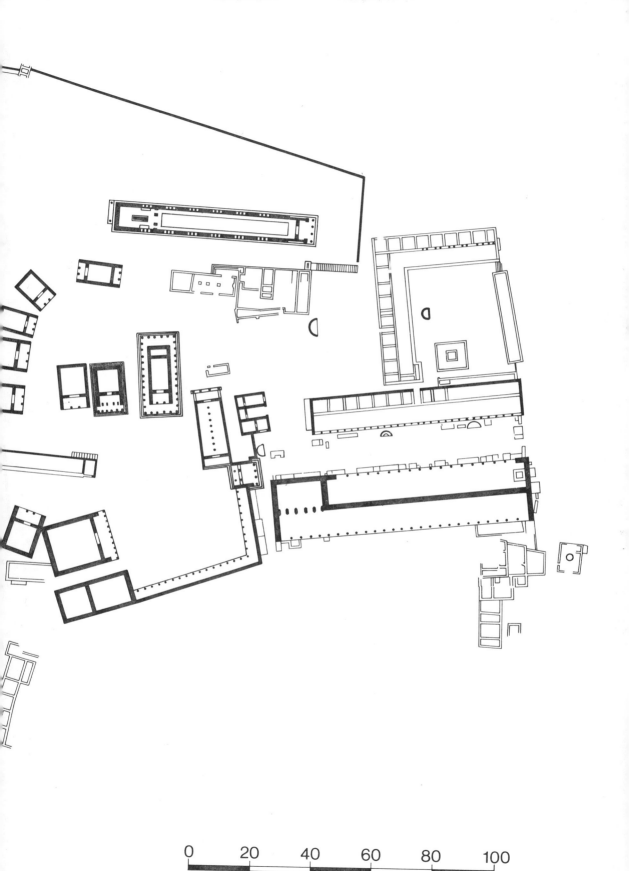

0   20   40   60   80   100

The earliest buildings here (apart from the foundations and deposits of the late Bronze Age) which are religious in character belong to the seventh century BC, when a temple-like structure was built by the people of Naxos. This was called the house (*oikos*) of the Naxians, and is unlikely to have been a temple in the functional sense. From this time the island flourished as a religious centre, and innumerable dedications and monuments were placed on it. These included a colossal marble statue of Apollo, fragments of which still survive, and which was placed in the open air (like an Egyptian colossus) not as a cult-statue in a temple. The best preserved of these early dedications is the series of hound-like lions standing on a terrace which overlooks the sanctuary (plate 19). These again recall, in a completely altered and Hellenized fashion, the avenues of Sphinxes which were common in Egyptian religious places, and which were now becoming known to the Greeks. During the seventh and sixth centuries, the sanctuary would appear to have been supported chiefly by the neighbouring Cycladic islands, perhaps dominated by Naxos. Whether this implies that it was the centre of a religious league, akin to that of the Amphiktyonic council of Delphi, or the league of the eastern Ionians of Asia and the off-shore islands, is not certain; nor, assuming that there was such a league, is it clear that it was anything other than religious in character or purpose, though it may have had or acquired some political significance.

During the sixth century Athens began to take a significant interest in Delos. The Athenians were recognized as a branch of the Ionian Greeks; indeed, they claimed to be the mother-city of the Ionians, the original state which established the Ionian colonies across the Aegean, and this gave them the right to participate in the religion of Apollo on Delos. It is not known when this participation, which involved the despatch of an Athenian warship to take the official representatives to the annual festival, first began. The claim that Athens was the mother-city of the Ionians was current at least as early as the beginning of the sixth century,[17] but it was later in the century, during the period when Athens was ruled by Peisistratos, that Athenian involvement in Delos first reached serious proportions. Herodotus desribes, first, how Peisistratos subdued the island of Naxos and established as its ruler his friend and ally Lygdamis; so this may have involved the ending of Naxian predominance on Delos. Next, Peisistratos went to Delos and purified the area that overlooked the sanctuary, digging up the dead and reburying them on another part of the island.

For the time being, this Athenian interest seems to have had no effect on the monumental arrangement of the sanctuary. The troubled times of the Persian involvement in the Aegean may be partly responsible, and in 490 the Persian fleet, sailing to attack Athens, deliberately put in at Delos to make offerings and pay the respects of the Persian king to the Ionian god, thus clearly indicating who was now the dominant power in the Aegean. No trace of these Persian offerings has survived. The fortunes of the island changed once more with the defeat of the Persians in 479. The Greek fleet—predominantly now the splendid new ships which Athens had completed just before the Persian attack in 480—had made Delos its advanced base for 479, covering the operations in Greece but poised to advance to the east Aegean when opportunity arose. When the Greeks decided to continue the naval alliance after 479 to protect themselves from any renewal of the Persian onslaught, the leadership fell to Athens (rather than Sparta, whose interests were more directly concerned with the mainland). Delos was chosen as the centre of the alliance, neutral ground sanctified by religious usage and particularly appropriate since the majority of members were Ionians. The alliance involved meetings of the allies, which took place regularly in the temple of Apollo. It also involved the collection of financial contributions for its military expenditure, and from these a tithe (to be precise, one sixtieth) was sacred to the god.

The architectural development of the sanctuary was slow (plate 20). A new temple to Apollo was started, more magnificent than the simple structure of the archaic age but not very large; it measures 40 feet 11 inches by 93 feet 7¼ inches (12.47 by 28.53 metres). It was to be peripteral, and, probably, planned in the Ionic order though built in the Doric.[18] Work had not progressed beyond the stonework when it came to a halt. There is no certain reason for this; it may possibly be the result first of the decision to transfer the treasury of the alliance from Delos to Athens in 454, after the island had suddenly become vulnerable to possible attack from a rebuilt Persian fleet, and secondly of the loss of a substantial part of the Greek fleet while trying to support an anti-Persian rebellion in Egypt. When the treasury was transferred it came instead under the protection of Athena: and it was she who henceforth received the tithe of one sixtieth. Possibly, without these funds, Delian Apollo could not afford to proceed with the construction of his temple; or, if it was the Athenians who were building it, they would now seem to have lost interest.

The real revival belongs to the period of the Peloponnesian war. Although work was abandoned on the buildings of the Acropolis and other Athenian sanctuaries there was more interest in Delos. The first part of the war had not gone well for Athens, and she had suffered particularly from the plague, an event inevitably attributed to the wrath of the gods. In 426 the Athenians carried out a new, more thorough purification of Delos. This would seem to have been coincidental with decrees tightening Athens' control over her Ionian and other allies; and it may be that the renewed activity in Delos was intended to emphasize Athens' claim to control through her religious supremacy. This time the purification was, as far as possible, complete; the corpses were removed to Rheneia, and the bans on death and childbirth were enforced. The Athenians also constructed a temple to Apollo, known as the temple of the Athenians. The fact that they did not attempt to complete the unfinished temple suggests that it was not begun under their auspices. The new temple is a curious building; the site for it was cramped, so that it could not have a full peristyle. Instead of a normal porch, there are internal piers separating the six columns of the façade from the cella, while the cella itself is largely taken up by a semicircular base, running across the back, which once supported seven statues; this appears to have been taken from the sixth-century temple and determined the width of the cella, 40 feet 11 inches (12.47 metres). As a result, there was no room for colonnades to either side, but the façade, and the rear, were each given six columns, so that the building appeared to be as impressive as its neighbour.

There is no overall plan or arrangement for the sanctuary, and no clearly defined boundary to it. There was a gateway in the south-west corner, by the early building of the Naxians. This led to a paved court, with other minor buildings, a shrine of Artemis, the colossal Apollo and a palm tree made of bronze, commemorating that on which Apollo's mother Leto leant when about to give birth to Apollo and his sister Artemis. The temples were on the eastern side of this area, and faced west. This area came to be enclosed, but, in view of the generally sacred nature of the island, it is not surprising that the next phase of development saw buildings constructed over a wider area.

During the fourth century the fortunes of Delos fluctuated. The defeat of Athens had brought independence, but this was short-lived; and it was only with the eventual decline of Athens that her strict control was relaxed and independence effectively restored (Athenian control was itself restored by the Romans in 167 BC, but by that time the development of the sanctuary was fully achieved). In the early Hellenistic period, Delos reverted to its role as the centre, based on religious importance, of an island league; the controlling force was now no longer the Athenian navy, but the ships and financial interests of the Macedonian kings who ruled Egypt, the dynasty founded by Ptolemy. The games inaugurated in honour of Ptolemy, the Ptolemeia, now became an important element in the religious life of the island. The great rivals of the Ptolemies for control of the Aegean, and with it the island of Delos, were the kings of Macedon itself, the descendants of Antigonos. Their eventual success led to the establishment of a different contest, the Antigoneia, together with much imposing building. This included a long enclosed hall, the roof beams supported on the inside of the walls by brackets decorated with bull's heads, and therefore known as the 'Hall of the Bulls'. Its long, narrow proportions make it almost certain that this was the shed in which one of the victorious Antigonids dedicated to Apollo the flagship of the fleet which had won for him victory over that of Ptolemy. The victory may be that of Antigonos I over Ptolemy I, fought under the command of Antigonos' son Demetrius at Salamis in Cyprus in 306 BC, or success in one of two sea battles his grandson, another Antigonos, fought against Ptolemy II about the middle of the third century.[19] The hall is situated to the east of the temples, and its length would have made it an effective visual barrier at this side. To the north of the sanctuary the younger Antigonos built an extended stoa almost 390 feet (119.93 metres) in length, terminating with gabled wings projecting forward, on the pattern first established by the stoa of Zeus at Athens (plate 21). To the south of the sanctuary the grandson of this Antigonos built his colonnade, only to have it deliberately obscured by that of a rival monarch, Attalos of Pergamon.

Other buildings are further afield. South of the sanctuary, beyond an area developed in Hellenistic times as a substantial town, is the theatre. To the north-east, a stadium was built. Other shrines, a temple of Isis, the courtyard cult-building of the worshippers of Poseidon of Berytus (Beirut) reflect the extended Greek world of Hellenistic times, and the importance of Delos in it.

Altogether, Delos does not have such spectacular temples as Delphi or Olympia. The complexities of the island sanctuary are achieved more by the irregular juxtaposition of smaller structures, devoid of balance, and emphasizing, more than Olympia with its open spacing, or Delphi with its dramatic approach, the haphazard nature of the forces which often predominate in the development of Greek sanctuaries. But above all, it too has a setting of beauty whether the Aegean is at rest or lashed to foaming waves (as it can be in midsummer) which break against the island's rocky northern end. Everything is to scale—the small island, the small mountain of a mere

300 feet which lies behind the sanctuary, the buildings of the sanctuary itself.

Compared with Delphi and Olympia, Delos ended early. The last two centuries of Hellenistic independence saw the development of the island as a wealthy trading centre, profiting particularly from the slave trade; this development was accelerated by the Romans after 167 BC when they promoted Delos as a trade rival to Rhodes, which had offended them. In the troubled times of the early first century BC the island was vulnerable to pirate attack. When Mithridates, King of Pontos, engaged in war with the Romans, Delos was a symbol of his enemy's interference in the affairs of Asia and the Aegean. With the king's encouragement, the pirates carried out a devastating raid in the island in 88 BC, from which it never really recovered.

6 Other important sanctuaries

The Acropolis, Athens

The Athenian Acropolis is a natural citadel (plate 22 and fig. 13). Steep sided and approached with comparative ease only from its western end, it formed the obvious stronghold for a population occupying the valleys of the two rivers, Kephisos and Ilissos, which flow to west and east of it. From the late Bronze Age it was fortified, the defences at the vulnerable western end being particularly massive; in all probability it was then crowned with a palace building similar to those at Tiryns and Mycenae. The approximate position for such a palace is known, and it is confidently marked on many plans of the Acropolis.[1] Its exact form and appearance, however, are quite uncertain. The massive fortifications belong to the thirteenth century BC; and towards the end of that century an elaborate arrangement was made to ensure that a water supply was available in case of siege, by way of a tunnel approached from the top of the Acropolis with a staircase.[2] The classical Athenians believed that their city escaped unscathed from the troubled times which followed the Trojan war. The archaeological record, on the other hand, suggests that Athens was at the least impoverished, along with the rest of Greece; and some distinguished scholars believe that newcomers replaced the original population.[3] This, however, is so directly opposed to the Athenians' own belief about themselves that it is surely preferable to find fault with the archaeological interpretation.

Athens is one of the cities of ancient Greece where continuity in the practice of religion from the Bronze Age to the historical period is a probability. Yet, again, there is no sound archaeological evidence for this, no sign of provable religious activity on the Acropolis until the eighth or seventh centuries BC. Throughout the intervening centuries the Acropolis served as a place of refuge, its fortifications still those of the late Bronze Age; but no trace survives of buildings, whether religious, administrative or residential. There are remains of houses outside the Acropolis, and it is probable that the Acropolis itself was not inhabited, except in an emergency; whether there were still kings at Athens, and whether, if so, they lived on the Acropolis, are moot points.

If there was religious continuity, it did not express itself in buildings. The evidence is less tangible than that of archaeology. To say that the classical Athenians believed that Athena was their protecting deity from a time long before the Trojan war means little, for legends can be manufactured; but this belief was enhanced by others, and sacred spots on the Acropolis itself, which make a late invention less likely. The story of the contest between Athena and Poseidon for the possession of Athens, the mark made on the Acropolis rock where Poseidon struck it with his trident, the sacred olive tree, Athena's gift to the city which won it for her, are part of a long-established

13 *Opposite*, the Acropolis, Athens

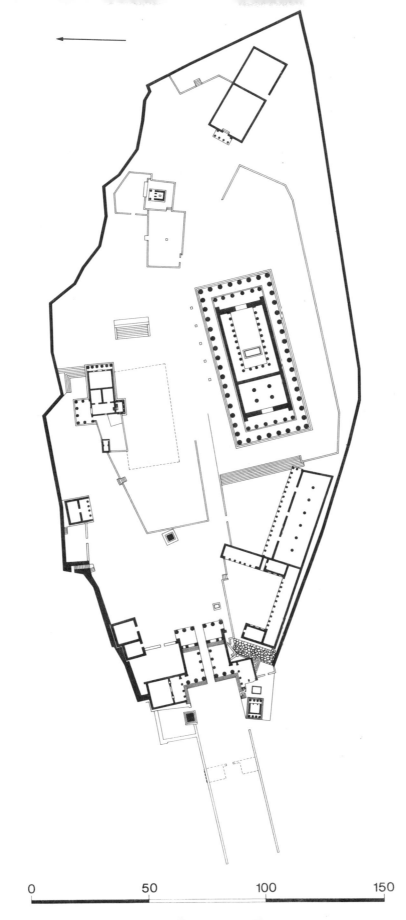

0   50   100   150

tradition.[4] At one point we seem to be in direct contact with the Bronze Age; though the staircase to the well had long since collapsed, the upper steps were still open from the Acropolis; each year maidens carrying mysterious bundles on their heads descended the remaining steps and returned, as part of an apparently meaningless ritual. We, since the excavation of the well, can see the origin of this, as a memory distorted with ritual of the way the women of the late thirteenth century descended the stair to obtain water.

Even so, the functioning of the Acropolis as a sanctuary does not become really clear until the seventh and sixth centuries BC. By that time, three essential elements can be defined. The entrance was at the old late Bronze Age gateway, flanked by the massive masonry of the fortifications (plate 23). Whether the gate itself survived from the Bronze Age, or whether it had been replaced at the beginning of this period by a new structure of the porch and cross-wall type, is difficult to decide; it certainly acquired an example of the latter in the sixth century. Even so, the alignment of the entrance was determined by the military needs of the late Bronze Age, not the religious purposes of the seventh or sixth centuries BC. The altar stood at the summit of the Acropolis, which is nearer the eastern than the western end. It was already there in the seventh century, when we hear of people taking refuge at it, and must have been much older than that.[5] We know nothing of its form; if it was structural, it was nevertheless simple, and it has left little trace at the present time.

The third element was the temple of Athena. This stood between the entrance and the altar (which it faced), on the presumed site of the Mycenaean palace. The placing of the three elements in relation to each other is partly fortuitous, determined by the survival of Bronze Age elements. The placing of the altar on the highest point of the Acropolis rock was more concerned with the requirements of cult, and the exact position of the temple was perhaps rather determined by the need for its east end to face the altar, than any exact memory or tradition of Bronze Age building. The architectural history of the temple is a matter of some controversy.[6] It was largely destroyed by the Persian invaders in 480–479; parts of its entablature were then dismantled, and built into the north wall of the Acropolis, apparently as a form of war memorial. Part of the structure called the *opisthodomos* or 'rear room' survived in a patched-up form as a treasury, and was demolished only after the rebuilding of the Acropolis in the late fifth century. The temple was taken down to its foundations, but these were left intact and are, indeed, still clearly visible on the Acropolis. In its final sixth-century form the temple was a peripteral Doric building of six by fourteen columns; within the colonnade the inner building had porches at either end, each of four columns placed in front of the termination of the side walls (*prostyle*) rather than between them, leading to separate eastern and western rooms; the latter presumably comprises the *opisthodomos*. It is generally assumed that this western part consisted of an ante-room and two inner chambers placed side by side. The details of the superstructure which have survived—the capitals and entablature built into the Acropolis wall—suggest that this temple was thoroughly reconstructed in about 525 BC. The foundations are of earlier workmanship, and it is clear that this temple was merely a replacement for an earlier one. Here, however, we are faced with greater uncertainty. A temple of about 600 BC is likely, and it has been argued that this was already peripteral. Since we now know that peripteral temples already existed at Corinth and

1 *Above*, Olympia: bases of monuments near the ruined temple of Zeus
2 *Below*, an example of the Doric order: the temple of Aphaia, Aigina
3 *Overleaf*, an example of the Ionic order: the temple of Nike, Athens

4 *Left*, the treasury of the Athenians, Delphi

5 *Below*, Brauron: dining-rooms, with some stone tables still in position

6 *Above*, fountain house: sanctuary of Zeus at Labraunda (Caria)
7 *Below*, Olympia: the Altis, looking from the temple of Zeus towards the temple of Hera

8 *Left*, Olympia: the vaulted passage, from the stadium
9 *Below*, Olympia: the temple of Hera

10 *Right*, Olympia: the terrace of the treasuries
11 *Below*, Olympia: east front of the temple of Zeus (left foreground: the tall base for the statue of Victory)
12 *Overleaf*, Olympia: columns of the palaistra

15 *Left*, Delphi: the pillar monument to King Prusias of Bithynia
16 *Below*, Delphi: theatre and
temple

17 *Above*, Delphi: the sanctuary
of Athena
18 *Right*, Delphi: the tholos in
the sanctuary of Athena

19 *Above*, Delos: Naxian lion
20 *Below*, Delos: general view of sanctuary, from the south-west

21 *Above*, Delos: part of the entablature, stoa of Antigonos
22 *Below*, Athens: the Acropolis, from the Hill of the Muses

23 *Above*, the Acropolis Bronze Age wall, with Parthenon in background
24 *Below*, the Parthenon: east end

25 *Above*, the Propylaia: from the west

26 *Right*, the Propylaia: north-west wing ('Pinakotheke')

27   *Above*, south-west pier of the
Propylaia, and temple of Nike
28   *Left*, the Erechtheion: the
north porch

29 *Above*, the Erechtheion:
from the south-east
30 *Right*, the Erechtheion: the
south porch (the Caryatids)

31 *Above*, the Parthenon: metope
sculpture *in situ*, and space where
another has been removed
32 *Left*, Isthmia: wall of the
seventh-century temple

33   *Right*, Epidauros: exedrai
34   *Below*, Epidauros: foundations of the 'thymele'

35 *Left*, Epidauros: supports for couches — great hall of the courtyard building

36 *Below*, Epidauros: the stadium

37 *Above*, Epidauros: the theatre
38 *Below*, Aigina: sanctuary of Aphaia, remains of the altar

39 *Above*, the sanctuary of Zeus, Nemea
40 *Left*, storage cistern, Perachora

41 *Above*, the temple of Apollo, Bassai
42 *Right*, the temple of Apollo, Bassai, interior

43 *Above*, the foundations of the temple of Athena Alea at Tegea
44 *Below*, Lykosoura: sanctuary of Despoina

Isthmia this is not unlikely. The chief doubt arises from the fact that the foundation of the outer colonnade is of a different material from that of the inner structure, and shows the use of a claw chisel in the preparation of its stonework. Thus the possibility that the colonnade is a later addition to the plan is attractive. A date of 525 BC, however, seems much too late for this, and it is more likely that we have an inner foundation belonging to the seventh century, the surrounding colonnade being added at about 600 BC.

Other elements in the arrangement of the archaic Acropolis are less certain. The temple stood on a platform which was supported towards the west by a terrace wall, of Bronze Age date. It is possible that this wall formed an inner boundary, defining the strict area of Athena's sanctuary from the general area of the Acropolis. This would be particularly necessary if the Acropolis was still used at this time for habitation. It has also been argued that if such an inner boundary existed it would have had its own propylon, of porch and cross-wall type; but this is entirely hypothetical. More serious is the problem of the second temple to Athena. When the Acropolis was rebuilt, it eventually carried two temples to Athena, the Ionic temple on the northern side, colloquially known as the Erechtheion, and the larger Doric temple on the south side, colloquially known as the Parthenon. The Erechtheion was officially described as the 'Old Temple', or, more fully, the 'temple in which the old image is'.[7] It is adjacent to the site of the archaic Doric temple just described, and quite clearly was intended as its replacement after the Persian destruction, housing as it did the sacred cult-statue (of wood) which the Athenians had then taken with them to Salamis when the city was evacuated.

The Parthenon, equally clearly, is a replacement, or rather resumption, of a large Doric temple which was begun about 490 BC, and only partly completed when the Persians captured Athens; the later temple incorporates much of its substructure and foundations, and reuses some of the superstructure. It has been argued that this earlier Parthenon itself was intended as a replacement for a temple on the same site belonging to the sixth century, probably about 565 BC, and that it was connected with the foundation, at that time, of the athletic contest, the Panathenaic festival.[8] The evidence for this is largely hypothetical; there are references to a 'hundred foot' temple which, it is argued, cannot be the old temple, since none of its dimensions conforms; there also exist the remains of large pedimental sculptures dating from about 565, which must come from some temple; the old temple was not, as far as we know, reconstructed at this time. The problem will never be satisfactorily resolved, since no one is likely to propose the demolition of the Parthenon to see what lies underneath it. It might be pointed out that 'hundred footer'—*hekatompedon*—as the description of a temple is, as we have seen, an indication of large size not of precise measurement, and could be applied to the old temple in its peripteral form; while the pediment sculptures could have come from a peripteral old temple, since replacement of this decoration need not involve any reconstruction of the architecture. The existence of a sixth-century predecessor to the Parthenon is extremely dubious.

The Acropolis was not entirely given over to the cult of Athena, as far as religious usage is concerned. On the bastion overlooking the entrance a cult of Nike (Victory) was established, while just inside the entrance, on the south side, an area was set aside for the cult of Artemis. This offshoot of her major sanctuary at Brauron, on the east side of Attica, was deliberately introduced in the sixth century by Peisistratos, who then controlled Athens and who had interests in that region (and, presumably, its local cult). The architectural development of these separate sanctuaries is best traced in the subsequent fifth century.

In the course of the sixth century the Acropolis had developed considerably, with splendid up-to-date buildings lavishly decorated. There were also many lesser monuments and private dedications, particularly marble statues. Limestone was still the principal building material, used, for example, in the old temple. The earlier sculptural decoration was also in limestone (several small pediment compositions have survived of the mid-sixth century which cannot be attributed to any particular building) but later in the century island marble was imported, and artists flocked to Athens from many parts of the Greek world. The latest pre-Persian buildings, on the other hand, the uncompleted predecessor of the Parthenon, and the ornamental porch and cross-wall gateway were built with superstructures of Pentelic marble, quarried in Attica on the slopes of Mount Pentelicus. When freshly quarried and trimmed this stone is a dazzling and brilliant white—the oxides which subsequently turn it to a golden honey colour would not be apparent until it has weathered, probably for centuries. It also allows superb precision of carving, and gives to the buildings constructed from it a crispness impossible in even the best hard limestone. It is evident that the first buildings of marble already demonstrate these qualities, and the full potential of the material.

The arrival of the Persians was not unexpected, and it was obvious to the Athenians that their defensive policy might require the evacuation of the city. That the Acropolis was expected to fall is proved by the way the Athenians took the most sacred image of Athena to Salamis, where it could be defended by the 'wooden walls' of the fleet.[9] Nevertheless the Acropolis was organized for defence, and a garrison left behind, supposedly of diehards who refused to believe that the wooden walls, which the Delphic oracle had promised would save Athens, were her ships rather than the wooden defences on the Acropolis. The story gives the impression of an improvised defensive system on the Acropolis, but this is misleading (as, perhaps, are most Greek stories pertaining to oracles) for the Acropolis still possessed its Bronze Age walls, the only modification being the alteration of the entrance to more decorative form. Probably the Athenians felt that their most sacred spot could not be given up without a fight, and some of them would have regarded surrender without a struggle as a betrayal of the goddess. Resistance may also have helped delay the Persians' plan for the next move in their conquest of Greece; but as a defence of the Acropolis it was in vain. The Persians stormed the citadel, and burnt the buildings on it. The statues were knocked from their pedestals and broken; the whole sanctuary was left a wilderness of destruction.

Nevertheless the Persians were eventually defeated, and the Athenians regained control of their city. The lower town, too, had been destroyed when the Persians finally gave up hope of winning the Athenians over to their side; and the problems of reconstruction were immense. Surprisingly little was done on the Acropolis, at least to the sanctuaries there. The 'back room' of the Old Temple was patched up, but this was to serve as a lockable treasury; the rest of the building was demolished, and the cult-statue, brought back from Salamis, was housed in a temporary shack by

its north-east corner, facing towards the altar. The broken statues and other fragments were tidied up; the statues, sacred to Athena, could not be thrown away, and
so were buried on the Acropolis itself, where they remained until they were unearthed
by nineteenth-century archaeologists. Reconstruction work was concerned first with
the repair and alteration of the circuit wall, for defensive rather than religious purposes. The failure to rebuild immediately the religious buildings is a little surprising.
The other public monuments of Athens, the administrative buildings and so forth,
had also been destroyed, but there were not many of them; in any case, they were
architecturally simple, and built from relatively inexpensive materials. Private houses
were equally simple, and it is unlikely that their reconstruction was a charge on the
state. In any case, Athens was not impoverished by the war, and the booty from the
campaign of 480 and 479, and the continuation of the war against the Persians, culmi-
nating in the victory of the Eurymedon in the early 460s, was not negligible. True,
the military or, rather, the naval effort required constant expenditure; but the lack
of religious reconstruction is still strange. In later times the Greeks themselves found
this puzzling, and explained it by an oath, taken before the battle of Plataea in 479, that
the ruins of the sanctuaries destroyed by the Persians would be left as a memorial to
the atrocities of the barbarians.[10]

The impetus for rebuilding came shortly after 450. The attempt by Athens to wrest
supremacy in the Greek mainland from Sparta was approaching its unsuccessful conclusion, to be terminated by the peace of 445. On the other hand, the maritime
struggle with Persia, revived in the mid-450s after a lull, had been more successful, the
Persian fleet being once more destroyed. Here Athens' hold over her maritime alliance
was assured, and the Spartans did not consider trying to take it from her. The rebuilding of the sanctuaries might have been to celebrate the victory over Persia, and this
argument would be supported if we could be certain that a formal peace was then
made with the Persians: this, unfortunately, is one of the great uncertainties of fifth-
century Greek history.[11] If we can believe in the peace, it might be that the Athenians
at Plataea took a vow not to rebuild the temples until the Persians were finally
defeated, and that this time had now come. Otherwise, the set-backs (and eventual
failure) against Sparta might have led the Athenians to attempt the winning of further
support from the gods by giving them new sanctuaries.

The reconstruction begins in a most minor way with a proposal to build a new
gate to the sanctuary of Victory (Nike), on the bastion by the entrance to the Acropolis. The evidence is in the text of a proposal passed by the Athenian assembly, and
inscribed on stone.[12] The inscription is not complete, and lacks the preamble which
would date it securely; but from the form of the letters used it appears to belong to
about 450 BC. Even when the proposal was made it was decided to draw up specifica-
tions for a more thorough reconstruction of the sanctuary; the architect assigned this
task was Kallikrates. Yet the sanctuary was not rebuilt until the 420s, by which time
much more had been done on the Acropolis; it seems that before reconstruction of
the Nike sanctuary could begin, a much more thorough reconstruction of the
Acropolis was approved, of which the Nike sanctuary would form only a minor part.

The rebuilding was carried out successively (though other building was being done
at the same time at other sanctuaries). Work started in 447 with the largest building,
the Parthenon. Next came the completely reconstructed and elaborated gateway, the

Propylaia, left unfinished in 431 with the renewal of war between Athens and Sparta. During a lull in the fighting the Nike sanctuary was at last taken in hand, and work started on the Erechtheion. Though the war was resumed, the building of the Erechtheion continued; it was completed (after a set-back caused by an accidental fire) in 406, just before the final defeat of Athens. The work was thus extended over more than forty years, and the possibility of some modifications in the original plan must be considered. It must be remembered that in more favourable circumstances work would have been completed with less delay; and it still seems best to consider this reconstruction essentially as the achievement of a single, unified plan for the amelioration of the Acropolis, not the haphazard adding of buildings without forethought over an interminable period.

The interest of the new arrangement derives partly from the way it overcomes the restrictions inevitable in a context which had been used for religious purposes for centuries. The architect who drew up the plan (the implication of the Nike inscription is that it was Kallikrates, but this cannot be confirmed) was placed under severe restrictions. There were many fixed points which were sanctified by religious usage, and could not be changed. In addition, though the principal buildings were either patched-up ruins or incomplete wrecks, there were other monuments which were intact—statues and other dedications placed on the Acropolis since the Persian destruction. The changes to the fundamental ground plan of the Acropolis were therefore few; but they were significant, and the redesigned buildings seem to have been more carefully related to it, in elevation and general design, as well as their positioning.[13]

The key to the new arrangement is the realization that the religious ceremonies were not merely the static performance of the sacrifice at the altar, but included— were initiated by—a solemn procession from the city outside into the shrine. There was therefore a line of progression, with appropriate stages; the approach to the Acropolis, the inevitable moment of pause at the gate, the entry onto the Acropolis, the first view of the temples, the approach to the altar, and so forth. These are inevitable in any sanctuary; the new Acropolis plan appears to give particular attention to the architectural setting in which they take place, and leads to a formal relationship between the areas and buildings concerned with them. Particularly important is the Propylaia, which is the link between the outer and inner world; and the relationships between the Propylaia and the altar as the place of sacrifice. The old Propylaia had been placed obliquely, looking towards and therefore obscured by the Nike bastion; an alignment determined, as we have seen, by the original defensive purpose which was now essentially discarded. The new entrance was turned so that its outer porch looked out over the approach from the lower town, while the inner gave on to the central axis of the Acropolis itself, instead of the adjacent edge. This created a vista along the Acropolis rock, providing, as it were, the backbone of the new scheme. The alignment was directly towards the altar; but the slope of the Acropolis would prevent a simple, direct view. The Propylaia led to an open area, the place where the first inner view of the sanctuary would be attained. Beyond that, the Old Temple ruins were badly placed. The opisthodomos of the Old Temple was on the axis; the old Parthenon would (if completed) have dominated from the right, and created a total imbalance. The decision was therefore taken to move the Old Temple from its original site to an adjacent one, immediately to the north; the central axis then passed between the two temples. This, theoretically, creates the risk of an uninteresting symmetry, but this was avoided by the striking difference in design of the two new temples, the Parthenon a large, regular Doric structure, the Erechtheion a dainty, totally irregular Ionic one.

The actual reconstruction began with the Parthenon (fig. 14). It might have seemed more natural to begin with the Old Temple, the original shrine, of which the opisthodomos was still standing. The old statue from that temple was housed, even if in an unimpressive structure, and the decision to go ahead with the Parthenon can be explained by the possibility that a decision had already been made to use the rear room to house the treasury, thus permitting the demolition of the old opisthodomos. There may have been controversy over the form and placing of the Erechtheion, while the Parthenon site was available and uncontroversial. It is more than probable that the earlier Parthenon was being built to commemorate the first victory the Athenians had won over the Persians in 490 at Marathon; the completion of this temple was particularly appropriate to the celebration of the final victory over the Persian army. Perhaps it was felt that there were still restrictions and misgivings about the rebuilding of the Old Temple, while these were less strong when it was a matter of completing a temple which had never been finished, or given its cult-statue. It is, indeed, possible that the decision to complete the Parthenon came before the full plan for the Acropolis was devised.

The new Parthenon was to be larger—slightly—than the old, 101 feet 3¾ inches by 228 feet 0⅜ inches, instead of 77 feet 2½ inches by 219 feet 7½ inches (30·88 by 69·50 metres instead of 23·53 by 66·94 metres); it was also to be more impressive when

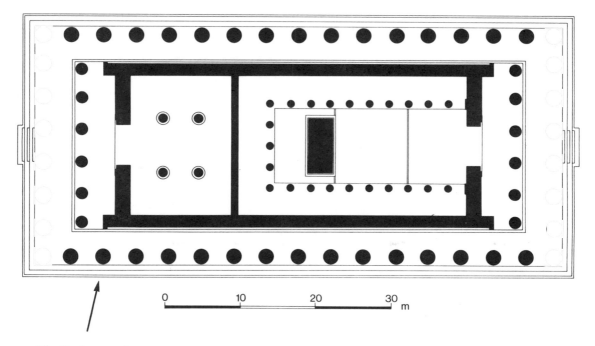

0   10   20   30 m

14 The Parthenon: plan

viewed from the ends, the sight that greets one on entering the Acropolis, by being given façades of eight rather than the original six columns (plate 24). This is not the place to analyse the details of the building itself, but there are several features which call for comment. The sculptural decorations emphasize the purpose of the building, its relationship with the cult of Athena, and the circumstances under which it was built. All ninety-two metope panels of the outer Doric frieze were carved with scenes of combat, Greeks against Trojans, Greeks against Centaurs, symbolizing the more recent struggle between Greece and the barbarian Persians. The pediment sculpture on the west end depicted the struggle between Athena and Poseidon for the patronage of Athens, a struggle which was supposed to have been enacted on the Acropolis itself; while on the principal, east end the sculpture represented the birth of Athena. In addition (and most abnormally) a continuous frieze of Ionic rather than Doric pattern was added extending from the entablature of the east and west porches along the top of the walls. This depicts the great Panathenaic procession—a perpetual record, as it were, of the part of the religious ritual which, we have argued, is essentially concerned with the new architectural arrangement of the Acropolis. It is interesting that the culmination of this procession is not the sacrifice of animals (though the animals are depicted on the frieze) but the offering of a new robe, woven by the Athenian maidens, to clothe the old cult-statue which was not in the Parthenon, but on the other side of the Acropolis. The Parthenon received the splendid statue of Athena by Pheidias, made from gold and ivory on a wooden frame. Despite its magnificence and costliness it never succeeded to the religious position of the old statue (and, indeed, it is unlikely that this was ever intended).

Another aspect of the Parthenon suggests more than religious significance. Before it was completed, the largest temple on the Greek mainland was that of Zeus at Olympia. The Parthenon outdoes it in all respects. It is slightly larger (the temple of Zeus measures 96 feet 10 inches by 210 feet $4\frac{1}{2}$ inches, 29·51 by 64·12 metres). It has eight instead of six columns to the façades. It has much more elaborate and extensive carved decoration. It was only after Pheidias was put on trial and banished from Athens that Olympia made some attempt to redress the balance by commissioning him to create a gold and ivory statue of Zeus.

If the temple at Olympia represents (as suggested above) a memorial to the joint effort of the Greeks in repelling the Persians, in which the Athenians played a part but under the leadership of Sparta, the Parthenon is more particularly to emphasize Athens' role after she has repudiated Spartan leadership. The rivalry between the temples was more than a matter of religious prestige; it symbolized the political rivalry between the two leading states of fifth-century Greece, and foreshadowed the devastating military conflict that was to ruin them both.

The second stage in the reconstruction of the Acropolis was directed to the Propylaia (plate 25). Here a more thorough reorganization was necessary. The gateway itself, placed at the top of the entrance but now moved onto the Acropolis axis, was probably much bigger than its predecessor (theories that the earlier Propylaia had a large structure have not received support).[14] The façades now consisted of six Doric columns, the central spacing being wider than the others. These stood on a stepped platform, but this was interrupted at the centre to give a passageway which could be traversed by the animals as well as the rest of the Panathenaic procession. The fore-hall was much deeper than that behind the cross-wall and required additional, inner support for the roof in the form of Ionic columns. There were five doors in the cross-wall; the largest, at the centre, would have been opened only for the processions. The rear hall was much shallower, and did not require inner supports; its floor level was higher, because of the rising slope of the Acropolis rock, and this difference in level was carried all the way up the building to the roof, though it is doubtful whether the awkward difference between the two sections would have been visible outside. Much stranger is the addition of other architectural elements on either flank of the main entrance building. The purpose and design of these has caused much controversy. That to the north of the fore-hall is the only section which includes a complete room. This has three smaller Doric columns in its porch and an off-centre door flanked by two windows (plate 26). It is described by Pausanias as a picture gallery; presumably it then contained panel pictures, but there are no traces of any provision for these.[15] The eccentric position of the door makes it very likely that it once contained couches, and served as a dining-room—there are no other provable dining-rooms on the summit of the Acropolis.[16]

On the opposite, south, side is a balancing porch of three Doric columns, with no room behind them. Instead, the side of the porch gives access to the Nike bastion. To north and south of the inner hall, indications in the structure—holes designed to receive beam-ends, a block modified to take the line of a non-existent roof—show that it was intended to add more rooms, but these were not built. Other indications such as unpolished surfaces to many wall blocks show that the Propylaia was abandoned, uncompleted, at the outbreak of war between Athens and Sparta in 431, and never resumed. It has been argued[17] that the south-west wing—balancing the 'dining-room'—is a truncation of the original intentions; that the first design was for a symmetrical façade, room balancing room, but that this had to be modified for religious reasons because it intruded into the precinct of Nike. It seems preferable here to take the view that the actual arrangement was intended from the first. It provides monumental access to the Nike bastion, which must have been an original purpose, and an appearance of quasi-symmetry—that is, the flanks seem to anyone approaching the Propylaia to be symmetrical, even if they are not so in plan. Here again it seems we have architecture designed from the point of view of the processions. The building as it were provides a theatrical illusion, as much as a monument to be admired in isolation. The function of the inner rooms, if they had been built, is even less clear. That to the north may have been intended to replace a set of simple, earlier rooms a little further round the Acropolis perimeter. That to the south would have been built largely within the sanctuary of Brauronian Artemis, and may have been intended to serve that cult. Neither of these rooms would have been concerned with the essential plan for the new visual approach to the main sanctuary, and, when building was resumed on the Acropolis, other construction was more urgent.

By the late 420s, it must have been clear to most Athenians that the war which they had provoked with Sparta was not moving to the success they had originally expected. The Athenians had in the meantime suffered the demoralizing effects of a plague, which normal religious attitudes would have attributed to the anger of the gods. The completion, so long delayed, of the temple to Victory on the bastion by the Propylaia is ironic in the circumstances. The temple itself is a delicate and small

Ionic building, with four columns to east and west (plate 27). Despite its small size, there is barely room for it on its platform—the west steps directly adjoin the sheer drop at the edge of the platform, though later in the fifth century a parapet, decorated with relief sculpture, was built round the bastion. To reduce the size of the temple, rather than omit the west colonnade (which, of course, gives the principal view of the structure), the cella and porch were collapsed into a single room, its entrance marked by two rectangular piers with metal grilles and a door between them, a device first used a year or two earlier in the Temple of the Athenians at Delos.

With a lull in the fighting it became possible to begin work on the new version of the 'old' temple, and religiously this must have been highly desirable. Even when the fighting was resumed, work on the new temple continued, in contrast to the earlier abandoning of the Propylaia. The new site for the temple was a most difficult one. It was not level, but, at the same time, it contained so many sacred spots that the usual method of building on an uneven site, the concealing of massive foundations beneath an artificial terrace, the method employed in fact in the construction of the Parthenon, was not here possible. These sacred spots include (besides the shrine of Erechtheus which gives the building its colloquial name) the sacred olive tree, the gift of Athena herself which won her the patronage of Athens in her contest with Poseidon, which had been cut down by the Persians and, miraculously, had grown again. It also included the mark on the Acropolis rock where Poseidon had struck with his trident, and which had thereafter contained a pool of salt water. The inclusion of these spots, most sacred to the religious traditions and worship of Athena, within a single structure must have been deliberate; indeed, the desire to do so may have been of itself a contributory factor in the decision to move the temple to a new site. The way the new building incorporates the salt pool of Poseidon is intriguing. It is situated in the north porch (plate 28), whose paving is interrupted to reveal the pool, while above a hole was left in the roof so that if Poseidon should ever decide to strike the Acropolis a second time with his trident, he could do so without damaging the Erechtheion!

The Erechtheion takes the irregularities of the Propylaia one stage further (plate 29). The core is the cella, a slightly reduced version of that contained in the Old Temple, with rooms facing east and west. These, however, are now on two different levels, the eastern at the higher level, the western at the lower. The east room contained the cult-statue and faced the altar; it had a façade of six Ionic columns. The lower level at the west end is concealed behind the wall surrounding Athena's olive tree, and the precinct of Pandrosos. It was thus possible to divide the west end in two, a plain lower section continuing the precinct wall, and an upper section with columns more or less on the level of those at the east end. This made it possible to balance the architectural details of the western and eastern ends, and to extend their Ionic frieze along the side of the cella. The main entrance to the western end had to be to the north, and consists of a large Ionic porch; but though its columns are bigger than those of the east porch they do not reach the same height, because of the difference in the ground level. They have their own entablature and roof, which abuts against the main cella structure. Even more awkwardly, the porch extends beyond the line of the west front, to include an entrance to the Pandrosos precinct. There is no structural necessity for this; the porch could easily have been placed a short distance to the east, to align its south wall with the south wall of the main structures, and the awkward position is adopted, therefore, out of deliberate choice, to link the entrance to the temple with the entrance to the sanctuary of Pandrosos, the area of the salt pool of Poseidon with that containing Athena's olive tree. The north porch is balanced by the much smaller south porch, directly opposite (plate 30). This is the famous porch of the maidens, where the columns are replaced by statues of sturdy young women, whose headpieces bear the weight of the entablature. This porch is necessarily at the higher level, but it gives access, by way of an angled staircase, to the west rooms at the lower level.

The total design is ingenious, rather than satisfying. The details, including the lavish decoration, are superb, but the total effect is again rather one of theatricality and illusion; the building is meant to be looked at from a distance, rather than inspected close to. Parts of it are rather disconcerting, particularly the porch of the maidens— perhaps intended to represent the maidens who descended the mysterious steps which were all that still remained of the Bronze Age well. It may be that, as part of the attempts to gather all the cults of this part of the Acropolis together in one building, it was now intended that they would go down the new staircase from their porch into the western room—a more meaningful action than the descent into a hole that led nowhere. Significantly, nowhere else was an attempt made to build a temple similar to the Erechtheion; it could only be built in this particular part of Athena's sanctuary on the Athenian Acropolis.

Thus the main form of the new arrangement was defined by these three buildings and the altar; and it is the ruins of the three fifth-century buildings which dominate the Acropolis at the present day. This would have been less obvious when they were first completed, for there were other monuments and buildings which would have complicated the arrangements, and even altered the emphasis. In the late fifth century a worshipper entering the Acropolis through the Propylaia would have had his attention drawn not so much to the temples as to the colossal bronze statue of Athena as the warrior goddess and protectress of Athens, an earlier work of Pheidias; so tall that it could be seen, and used as a landmark, from ships approaching the harbour at Piraeus five miles away. The position of this statue on the alignment between the Propylaia and the altar must be considered an integral part of the general design. To the south of the alignment, between the Propylaia and the Parthenon, were the sanctuary of Brauronian Artemis and an area called the Chalkotheke or armoury, where the suits of bronze infantry armour which were part of the regular offering to Athena were stored. Neither was of any architectural merit or importance; but their walls, entrances and colonnades modified the direct view, particularly of the Parthenon, and filled what nowadays appears rather as an open space. The number of smaller structures reduced the visible space, providing a setting quite different from that which appears today. The contrast in scale between these buildings and the major monuments would have made the temples appear even larger, more magnificent and lavish. There would have been considerably more variety than there now appears to be and a greater contrast of colour, for in addition to the grey of the Acropolis limestone and the white of the Pentelic marble, much of the sculpture (plate 31) and architectural detail was enhanced with blue and red paint; there was the glistening bronze of statues and other monuments—and, probably, more earth with flowers over the poor bare bones of the Acropolis rock. The crowded arrangement, with the organized plan as a backbone, must have given a much more exciting experience than anything which can be directly appreciated on the Acropolis at the present day.

Athens continued to flourish in the Roman period, and the religious observances on the Acropolis continued. In the first century BC a fire once again devastated the Erechtheion, but it was carefully repaired, the later craftsmen following the old patterns and demonstrating much of the skill of their fifth-century predecessors. The reconstruction provided the model for the only Roman addition to the buildings of the Acropolis, a small circular Ionic structure, its details based entirely on those of the Erechtheion, placed in front of the Parthenon and dedicated to the cult of Rome and the emperor Augustus. The Acropolis, unaffected by earthquakes, remained intact and in use as a sanctuary to the very end of the pagan period.

The Argive Heraion

During the late Bronze Age the Argive plain had been one of the principal centres of wealth and power, perhaps the principal centre, if the Homeric narrative which makes Agamemnon of Mycenae overlord of all Greece is based on fact.[18] Its advantage was the direct access to the Aegean and the trade routes to the East Mediterranean. At the end of the Bronze Age it suffered massive destruction and consequent depopulation, and never regained its former primacy. Nevertheless the region recovered steadily during the tenth and ninth centuries, and in the eighth century reached a high degree of prosperity. In the Bronze Age the principal centres had been at Mycenae and Tiryns, on the eastern side of the Argive plain. After the Bronze Age the centre of power shifted to Argos, on the western side, where there was an important settlement of immigrant Dorians, whose military prowess gave them political supremacy over the entire region.

The town of Argos had its own sanctuaries; the chief one, that of Apollo Lykeios by the Agora, is really known only from the literary sources, principally Pausanias.[19] The most important cult centre of the Argolid was on the opposite, eastern side of the plain, on a site which was used as a place of burial in the late Bronze Age.[20] No Bronze Age cult can be proved to have existed here, though objects found might indicate this. As usual, there is no evidence for continuity through the Dark Age. The sanctuary is that of Hera, whom Homer recognizes already as the principal divinity of the pre-Dorian Argolid; the cult belongs to the entire district, not merely Argos town. The ritual was administered by a priestess, who would seem to have been appointed for life. The qualifications for this office are uncertain; she may have been a member of the Dorian ascendancy of Argos town, but Hellanikos, who compiled a list of the priestesses in the fifth century, was able to trace them back to the Bronze Age, long before the arrival of the Dorians, though the reliability of his list is open to serious doubt.

The sanctuary is situated at a point where the hills which form the eastern boundary of the Argive plain begin to rise from the good agricultural levels, and where there were springs. The earliest visible feature (and, strangely, now that the sanctuary is so completely ruined, the most prominent of the remains) is a massive terrace support wall, built out of large boulders, but in a rough and rather unsophisticated manner which is not really reminiscent of the massive style of masonry used in the fortifications of the local late Bronze Age citadels. The wall is dated by the material in the fill behind it to the late eighth or early seventh century BC. In view of the scale of this work it is most likely that the sanctuary was already well established; but the excavations (carried out many years ago, and deficient in several respects) did not produce any firm evidence for the earlier occupation. The terrace platform was of considerable size, partly natural, partly artificial. It was paved with slabs of stone, on which the temple and altar rested. Very little remains of the temple; its plan and early history cannot be recovered. Part of the single step on which a surrounding colonnade was placed survives, as well as the wall footings; it seems likely that the superstructure was of unbaked brick, and the columns wooden, and, if so, could well be earlier than the mid-seventh-century stone temples at Corinth and Isthmia (close to Argos, and which the Argive architects must surely have known if they were built before the temple of Hera). There is a possibility that a smaller, simpler temple was built first, and later replaced by, or incorporated into, the peripteral structure; but this is only a hypothesis and is not essential to the explanation of the architectural sequence. There can be little doubt that the peripteral temple is one of the oldest substantial and monumental religious buildings of mainland Greece, and a landmark in the history of Greek architecture.

The interpretation of the surrounding sanctuary is also made difficult by problems of chronology. There are no other traces of building on the temple platform, though the former existence here of an altar is most probable. Other buildings developed in the area below the terrace wall. These include colonnades under the terrace wall which turn their back on the temple platform and look out over the Argive plain; one of these, at least, could belong to the earlier period of the sanctuary's development. Another building which has been given (doubtfully) an early date is a little to the west of this lower area; it is a courtyard building, containing three rooms with the remains of couches in them, which certainly provided a formal place for dining. It has been dated by the early Doric capitals found in it, which are presumed to belong to the columns of its courtyard, but it is just possible that these are accidental intruders, and that the real date of the building is somewhat later. There is no formal propylaia to the sanctuary. We know, from surviving legends, that the priestess was expected to make her way across the plain to the sanctuary from her home (presumably in or near Argos itself). It is possible that there was a sacred procession, which approached along a road below the sanctuary, turned, and then passed from west to east below the terrace, to reach the platform by the slopes at its eastern end. The colonnade would then have been placed to provide a covered vantage point from which the procession could be watched as it approached the sanctuary. From a relatively early time the sanctuary had a developed architectural response to the formal, ritual needs.

This arrangement held good until the fifth century BC. Small monuments and dedications were added in the area below the temple terrace, but these did not profoundly alter its appearance. During the sixth century Argive prosperity and fortunes were in decline; at one stage, the sanctuary witnessed the intrusion of an invading Spartan king and his army.[21] The original temple survived, apparently unaltered throughout this period. Despite its outdated and antique appearance, it was not replaced, though this is not in itself surprising, nor was any attempt made to add to the sanctuary a new temple in the established style of the late sixth century.

By the middle of the fifth century Argos was beginning to prosper again, and a peace concluded with Sparta in 451 BC guaranteed her tranquillity. A programme to extend and bring the sanctuary up to date was started. It would seem that this had already begun when the old temple was destroyed accidentally by fire in 423 BC. It has been suggested that the redevelopment of the sanctuary began much earlier than this, at about the middle of the fifth century, but that work was then delayed by the loss of craftsmen to the great Athenian building programme.[22] This is possible, but perhaps it is simpler to suppose that the work began after the cessation of the Athenian building programme on the outbreak of the Peloponnesian war when Argos, alone of the major states of mainland Greece, remained at peace. Since a new temple platform was created, it does seem that the original intention was to preserve the old temple, and that this plan was thwarted only by the accident of the fire.

The new addition to the sanctuary was to be essentially a repetition of the older one on the slightly lower level in front of it. A new support wall for this terrace was constructed, this time of ashlar blocks arranged in a step formation against a slope, rather than as a vertical wall. Part of this was occupied by a new, outward-facing colonnade, in the same relative position to the new temple as the original one was to the old. The steps also provided vantage points for spectators looking out over the approach to the sanctuary, either at processions or, as appears to have been the case with the rather similar steps at the sanctuary of Herakles on Thasos, to watch an area where athletic contests of some sort were held. The courtyard building with the dining-rooms was certainly in existence by the time of these developments, for the support wall makes a sharp change of alignment (and becomes a conventional vertical wall) in order to avoid it. On the new platform the new temple was a conventional Doric structure, influenced, it would seem, by the recent temple building in Athens and Attica. Apart from fragments of the superstructure, which included carved metopes and pedimental sculpture, only the bare foundations of the temple survive. Some of the inner detailing of the temple is obscure; it may be that, despite the Athenian influence, the metope decoration was restricted to the entablature over the interior columns of porch and false porch, that is, in the Peloponnesian manner of the temple of Zeus at Olympia. A large altar was eventually built (perhaps not till Hellenistic times, and therefore presumably replacing an earlier structure). This was a wide, elongated structure extending for the greater part of the width of the temple itself.

Apart from this (and some ill-understood Roman bathing buildings) there seems to have been no development in the sanctuary after the fifth century BC. The area was considerably impoverished in the fourth century, and perhaps suffered more than the adjacent regions. In Hellenistic times Argos was controlled mostly by a local dynasty of autocrats; and at the time when Hellenistic wealth might have led to further building, local interest seems to have been diverted towards the sanctuary of Asklepios in the neighbouring territory of Epidauros. In many other ways the sanctuary of the Argive Heraion seems to represent a case of arrested development, a sanctuary which served a local purpose, and for which a clear definition of function was arrived at in the very first stages of monumental architecture in Greece. Once this initial impetus was over, the Argives were satisfied with the arrangement, and, when the time came to rebuild, could do no more than repeat the existing pattern. In a strange way, the history of the sanctuary seems to reflect the history of the Argives themselves.

Isthmia

Poseidon's sanctuary at Isthmia was in the territory forming part of the city of Corinth.[23] It stands on the eastern slopes of the Isthmus which links northern Greece to the Peloponnese, and separates the Gulf of Corinth from the Saronic Gulf. The historian Thucydides remarks on Corinth's favourable position, at the junction of trade routes; and it was entirely appropriate that the sanctuary on the Isthmus, where Corinth was able to take advantage of sea routes to the west, along the Corinthian gulf, and to the east, by the Saronic gulf, was dedicated to Poseidon, god of the sea. (It might also be remarked that Poseidon is also the god of the earthquake, and that the Isthmus is a part of Greece distinctly prone to earth tremors.) The festival of Poseidon at Isthmia also became famous as one of the four major athletic contests of classical Greece, on a par with Olympia, Delphi and Nemea, and drew participants from a wide area, though the sanctuary never became a fully international one in the way that Olympia and Delphi did; presumably this was only possible where the controlling city was itself unimportant, while Corinth was one of the foremost cities of Greece.

Corinthian trade began to be important towards the end of the eighth century BC, when she was controlled by a dominant Dorian clan known as the Bacchiadai. Her pottery, which earlier had not been particularly significant either in quantity or artistic merit, became abundant and showed not only a pioneering adaptation of new ideas and motifs assimilated from the Near East, but also considerable achievement and originality in its own right. It is hardly surprising that at the same time Corinth was in the forefront of architectural development, and that her two temples of the first half of the seventh century, the older temple of Apollo at Corinth itself, and the first temple of Poseidon at Isthmia, are the first major stone buildings in peninsular Greece.

The plan of the early temple at Isthmia has been reconstructed on the basis of cuttings made in the rock to receive the foundations, the positions of the internal line of columns, and the marks of the scaffolding poles. Fragments of the superstructure— wall blocks, entablature fragments and tiles—also help in the reconstruction even though certain details inevitably remain conjectural, particularly where the later temple built on the same site has obliterated earlier details and markings. It is extremely fortunate that so much did remain unobliterated, and that the excavation was carried out with consummate skill; one wonders how much has passed undetected beneath other temples. As restored, the temple has a long narrow cella with a deep porch at its east end, and no false porch at the west. It was surrounded by a colonnade of seven by nineteen wooden columns. There was a single, internal row of columns to support the ridge. In plan this temple is not dissimilar to the early temples of Hera in Samos; sufficiently so to emphasize the essentially common origin of both mainland Doric and east Greek Ionic structures. The elongated plan of the cella is similar to that of other early temples in Greece, and is an obvious antecedent for the long, narrow cellas, without a false porch at the end, found in the early temples of the Greek west.[24] The constructional details of the superstructure are extremely interesting for the evidence they provide of the earliest stages of Greek stone-building techniques, though it is not possible to make a restoration of the temple elevation. Though the columns were still

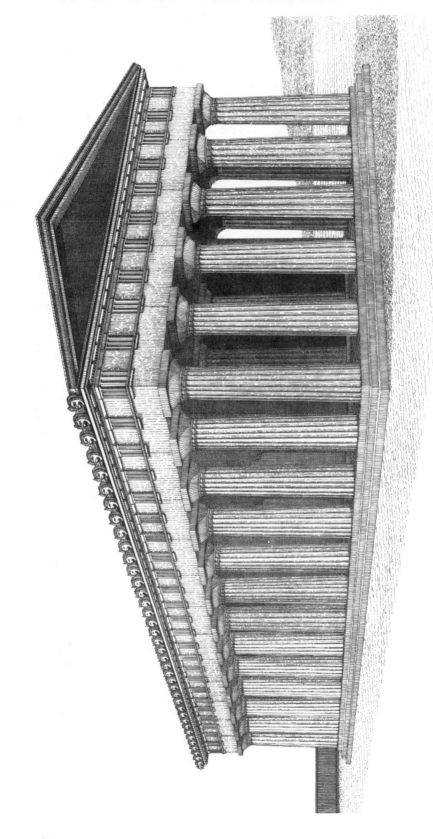

15 Reconstructed perspective: the fifth-century temple at Isthmia (based on plans and details by W. B. Dinsmoor, Jnr)

of wood, there is one stone column, probably a later replacement. The curious patterning on the wall surfaces, perhaps originating in mud-brick walls with embedded timber framing, has been remarked on already. The tiles were of the Corinthian type, though with slightly curved rather than flat pantiles. Specially shaped tiles from an angle indicate a hipped roof, at least at one end, and, since there is no sign among the not inconsiderable quantity of tile which has survived of the shaped tiles required to cover a pediment cornice, it is probable that the roof was hipped at both ends. The construction was mixed; the cornice, of stone, seems to have had timber facing. With wooden columns the entablature was also of wood, and there are no signs of terracotta revetments or metope panels.

This temple seems to have been destroyed in the early part of the fifth century, and probably by accident; there are distinct traces of burning in the surviving stonework. It is unlikely that the destruction was connected with the Persian invasion, which hardly reached the Isthmus. The temple was then rebuilt in a conventional mid-fifth-century Doric style, six by thirteen columns with a shallower Doric porch and a false porch at the rear, but still a single row of inner columns (fig. 15). This temple also was accidentally damaged by fire in an incident recorded by Xenophon in his *Hellenica* in the year 390. It was then repaired, to the same plan except that there were now the more normal two rows of inner columns (though these may have replaced the single row before the fire). In this final form it apparently stood until demolished for the late Roman fortifications across the Isthmus.

The arrangements of the sanctuary round the temple are not without interest. The temple itself is now in a sadly reduced state (plate 32); the superstructure has gone, and much of the foundations, leaving only the shallow trenches cut into the rock to take the foundation blocks. Around the temple are the remains of a rectangular courtyard, enclosed with a portico, which at the present is almost as conspicuous as the temple itself. This, however, is a later addition, of the Roman period. The classical sanctuary appears to have been open, and without a propylon. In front of the second temple are the foundations of the altar, of the long narrow type favoured in Corinthia and the Argolid. Only the foundations of this remain, and no restoration of its superstructure is possible; it may have been of the triglyph type, but this is quite uncertain. It was considerably wider than the temple, about 130 feet (40 metres) to the temple's 75 feet (22·90 metres). There is no trace of a built predecessor; it could have been on the site of the second altar, and so completely removed. Areas of ash and animal bones in the archaic level, and with a total width of 40 metres, suggest that there was an altar comparable with that of the later temple and in approximately the same area.

The sanctuary also contains a substantial theatre to the north-east of the temple area, well away from the most strictly sacred area (assuming that this, if not marked by a wall, at least corresponded approximately with the later Roman enclosure). The theatre is conventional in type, with considerable Roman modifications. Behind it, cut into the soft limestone so common in the Isthmian area, is a curious series of caves, possibly natural in origin, but certainly enhanced and enlarged artificially. These contained low rock-cut couches, and appear to have been the Isthmian equivalent of the formal dining-rooms found in other sanctuaries. The caves seem to have been arranged in interconnecting pairs, each pair having the total of eleven couches so common in the dining-rooms. The most curious feature of all was found just to the south-east of the temple, and subsequently obliterated by the Roman enclosure. This consisted of a line of holes intended to hold wooden posts, with a series of grooves cut in the rock surface behind them, coming together at a central point where there was a larger hole in the rock. There were also bronze loops in these grooves. This feature caused much puzzlement when it was first discovered, but it was soon interpreted as an arrangement for a starting gate for races. The posts supported hinged barriers, held up by strings which ran down the posts, through the bronze loops, and along the grooves to the central hole. Here they were held by a man positioned in the hole. By releasing all the strings together, the starting gates all opened simultaneously, enabling a fair start to be made to the race. It seems strange that such an ingenious device was not used more frequently in ancient Greece. The running area of the stadium extended to the south-east, away from the temple. It had none of the elaborate arrangements for spectators of the developed stadium, and is an interesting example of the very close relationship possible, before specialized architectural forms, between athletic activities and the sanctuaries. Later the area for athletic contests was moved to a conventional stadium in a valley further to the south-east. This has been excavated only in part, but the natural shape of the valley betrays its former function.

Other features of the sanctuary have less individual importance. There was a small shrine of Palaimon, which, Pausanias tells us, once contained statues of Poseidon and Leukothea, as well as Palaimon himself. To the south of the temple, and outside the later Roman precinct, is a large, circular pit, of uncertain function. A final feature to be noted is the existence of quite elaborate arrangements to provide a water supply to the sanctuary. There are excellent springs not too far distant, but water was brought into the area of the sanctuary itself from reservoirs by a series of piped conduits which can still be seen crossing the sanctuary area. Many of these are of Roman date but some are earlier; one, which makes use of the marble cover tiles discarded when the fifth-century temple was damaged by fire, seems to be early Hellenistic in date, perhaps the work of Demetrius Poliorcetes, who also seems to have been responsible for the provision of an even more elaborate system for water supplies at Perachora.

Epidauros

The city-state of Epidauros is bordered on the west by Corinth and Argos. A Dorian community, it was a small and rather insignificant place. The city itself was situated on the south coast of the Saronic gulf; behind was a sweep of cultivable land, none of really good quality, but pleasantly undulating. During the fourth century BC a large and important sanctuary of the healing god Asklepios was developed in the southern part of Epidaurian territory, well inland and away from the city on the coast. It lies in a sheltered, wooded and well-watered spot, naturally peaceful and rural, its restfulness now disturbed only by the modern tourist traffic which has inevitably developed.

The cult of Asklepios is of strangely late development.[25] Asklepios was recognized as a human being who had acquired fully divine status, rather than as one of the traditional Olympian deities. His cult was concerned with the well-being of the individual

16 *Opposite*, the sanctuary, Epidauros (after G. Roux, *L'architecture de l'Argolide*)

(rather than the community in general) and gained a special significance in the more troubled times of the late fifth century and after, when cities were often divided by class struggle, and the traditional pattern of life was increasingly disturbed. At this time sanctuaries of Asklepios were developed in Athens and Corinth in the Greek mainland;[26] but his principal mainland sanctuary was at Epidauros. As a relative late-comer to the Greek pantheon Asklepios did not possess sanctuaries traditionally dedicated to him and he was therefore accommodated in or near sanctuaries of other gods, particularly if they already had some healing significance. At Epidauros he was established by a small sanctuary of Apollo, but this was eclipsed by the new god.[27]

The sanctuary was developed below the earlier one to Apollo, where the road coming up from the coast and the city turned to approach it (fig. 16). The area occupied is reasonably flat, approached by a gentle incline from the north; to east and south are steeper sided hills. The development was undertaken by the Epidaurian state, and its principal citizens were involved. It is unlikely to have been a purely local effort, for the scale of development was probably well beyond the limited resources of the small city. Since it attracted worshippers from a wider area, it is likely that it also attracted funds. The earliest substantial building belongs to the 370s; and the sanctuary was virtually complete within a century. Unlike many Greek sanctuaries it continued to flourish in the Roman period, and even underwent some redevelopment then; but the sanctuary in its essentials is the creation of the fourth century BC, though the cult was established there some time before this. It is possible that this, the lower sanctuary (to distinguish it from the neighbouring upper sanctuary of Apollo Maleatis), was itself originally dedicated to Apollo alone, or possibly Apollo jointly with his son Asklepios. The cult of Asklepios was first centred on a square courtyard building, of no architectural pretensions, which included a shrine, an altar, and a place where the sick could sleep, to be visited by the god during the night in the form of a snake; the healing process was essentially achieved through this particular ritual of *incubation*. In about 430 Apollo left the lower sanctuary, his cult being concentrated in the upper area; and Asklepios remained with the healing cult. The courtyard building was perhaps regarded as his original home; but as the cult developed, the need for more building was felt.

The area was not, then, completely vacant; there was the original home, a well from which water for healing purposes could be drawn, and perhaps an adjacent bath building. But these structures were few, and there was considerable space for expansion. The resulting location of buildings seems haphazard, and it is argued that there was no overall plan for its development. Buildings bear no apparent relationship with each other, and there is no single alignment for them. Nevertheless the principles on which the sanctuary developed seem clear enough. The unifying feature must have been the road. As this approaches the sanctuary, it crosses a small stream, which appears to have marked the boundary, the beginning of the religious area. Here, subsequently, a sumptuous propylon was constructed which, nevertheless, seems to have served only a ceremonial and monumental purpose, for it can easily be passed to either side and had no closeable doors. It is some distance—at least 650 feet (200 metres)—from the main part of the sanctuary, which would not be much in view even when its buildings were intact because of the rising slope (at present, with the buildings reduced to little more than foundations, nothing can be seen). Later build-

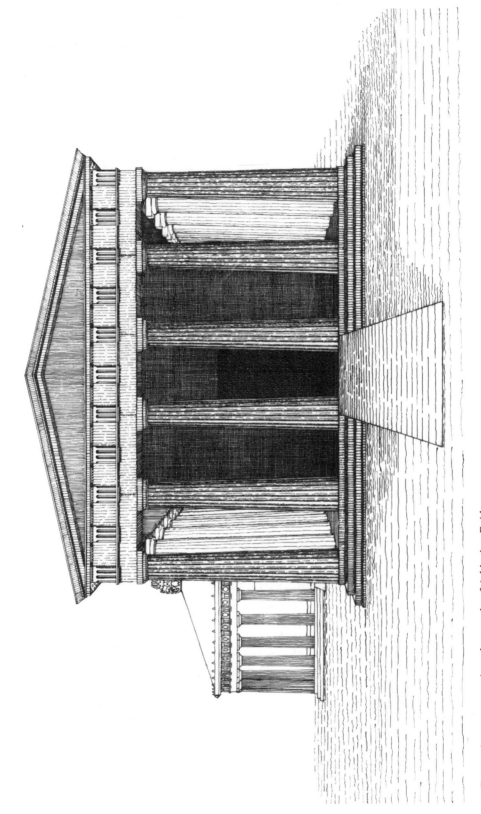

17 Perspective reconstruction: the temple of Asklepios, Epidauros (omitting sculptural decoration) with the thymele in the background

ings between the propylon and the centre of the sanctuary bridged this visual gap. At the top of the slope the road is enlarged to form a broad rectangular forecourt. Its northern boundary (that nearest the propylon) was marked by the construction of a colonnade, the 'Stoa of Kotys'. Otherwise it is open, and defined rather by a series of rectangular and curved exedrai, systematically and carefully placed, an excellent example of the use of such minor monuments for an architectural purpose (plate 33).

Beyond this court the road makes its way between the temple of Asklepios, to the west, and the old courtyard building, to the east. This involves a slight change of alignment, the road turning a little towards the east. This change is already noticeable in the alignment of the old courtyard building, a sure indication that the sanctuary grew up round an existing road. Beyond this, the road passes behind a temple of Artemis, and then, probably, along the west side of a very large courtyard building. The entrance to this, of monumental proportions, is at the western end of the north side, that is, immediately adjacent to the road. The building, normally referred to as a gymnasium, was undoubtedly used for ceremonial purposes involving a procession (for its entrance includes a ramp), while most of the rooms surrounding the court served as dining-rooms.[28] To the west of this, and not on a clearly defined route though the road must have turned here to go towards the sanctuary of Apollo, are a building apparently providing sleeping accommodation and, finally, the splendid theatre, the only one of the sanctuary's monuments which is at all well preserved.

Thus the important centre of the sanctuary is quite clearly defined, and the principal buildings were placed in relationship with it. This does not, of course, amount to a formal preconceived plan, but the definition of the various areas in the sanctuary was basic to the location of the structures. Within the central area itself the relationship seems more to have been functional than aesthetic. The essential principle was to establish a succession of movement from area to area and building to building in accordance with the various stages of what must have been a quite complex ritual. The sanctuary had to accommodate the sacred processions and altar sacrifices common to most Greek cults; but it also had to make provision for the healing ritual of incubation and a much greater emphasis on ritual feasting. In addition, the central part of the sanctuary includes a circular building, the tholos, superbly built and decorated, which was not a conventional temple, and which obviously played an important, but hotly debated, role in the cult of Asklepios. One result of this diversity is that the temple does not dominate the sanctuary architecturally, in the same way, say, that the Parthenon dominates the Athenian Acropolis.

The temple itself is a conventional Doric structure of the abbreviated form which became common in the fourth century BC, that is, without a false porch at the rear and with the number of flank columns reduced to eleven (fig. 17). It was built of imported stone, limestones of various types from Corinth and the Argolid; the use of marble (Pentelic, from Attica) was restricted to the carved decoration in the pediments and elsewhere. As was usual in Peloponnesian Doric temples, only the inner metopes of the porch were given carved decoration. There was also a decorative internal colonnade against the side walls; it has been suggested that this was already of Corinthian columns (which were certainly to be used in slightly later buildings at Epidauros, and elsewhere in the Peloponnese in the fourth century) but not enough of them has survived to provide clear evidence.[29] The temple was approached (as were all the

99

principal buildings in the sanctuary) by a ramp. It contained a gold and ivory cult-statue, the work of Arignotos of Paros. The temple was built quickly; the epigraphic evidence suggests in the surprisingly short space of four years and eight months, the length of time for which the architect Theodotos was paid. The rapidity of construction was made possible by the availability of funds, the small size of the building, and the easily worked limestone employed. The precise date of construction is less certain. It must fall within the period 390–370, and recent studies have suggested 375–370 as the most probable time.[30] The altar was placed in front of the temple, but north of centre, because of the location of the earlier courtyard building. It is on the other side of the route through the sanctuary; the forecourt would have provided a good place for worshippers to view the ritual of sacrifice.

Immediately beyond the temple, its front in exact alignment with it and facing the courtyard building, was another altar, probably belonging originally to Apollo. It is older than the temple, and has clearly influenced its position. Even more importantly, it is in direct axial alignment with the tholos, and must be responsible for the positioning of that structure also. The area round this forms a natural platform, as it were, level with the forecourt area, but sloping down to north, west and south. The circular tholos has an external Doric and an internal free-standing Corinthian colonnade. These, and the main wall, rest on circular foundation walls; there is a final, innermost foundation wall supporting the floor and defining a central pit. The spaces between these foundation walls are linked by doorways through the foundations (plate 34). In the inscriptions referring to its construction it is called the *thymele*, a word meaning 'hearth'. Its precise function remains an enigma; its importance is emphasized by its position, and the lavishness of its decoration.[31] Various suggestions have been made; that it is the cenotaph of Asklepios, the man who died and became a god; that it was a place of offerings (hardly burnt offerings, despite the connotation of a hearth, since there is no trace of fire in the structure), presumably to underworld forces and so made at the central pit; that it housed the sacred snakes used in the ritual of healing. The alignment with the old altar suggests that it was not merely an administrative or ancillary building, and the form of the structure supports this. Our ignorance of its precise function is evidence of our ignorance of Asklepian ritual. We have seen, though, that the circular building at Olympia commemorated a dead man, Philip of Macedon; and it is remarkable that other sanctuaries of Asklepios do not include similar structures. There was a pit of sacrifices in the sanctuary at Athens, but that is all. This suggests that the thymele at Epidauros is a special structure, relating to this particular sanctuary, and that it served particularly to link the sanctuary with the presence of Asklepios himself in a way that was not to be achieved by the more normal concept of the temple. There is no reason why all three of the functions suggested above, or some of them, could not have been involved in this single structure.

The construction seems to have begun soon after the temple was completed (particularly if we accept the date of 375–370 for the temple). This in turn suggests a close connection with the essential cult of Asklepios. This time, however, building work was protracted, for the thymele was not completed for at least twenty-seven years. The design was complex and original, and would naturally proceed more slowly than a straightforward temple. The decoration was lavish and intricate. The real reason for the delay, however, is more likely to have been the rapid deterioration in economic prosperity which affected Greece in general and the region round Epidauros in particular in the period after about 360 BC. It is not correct to argue that the slowness of construction means that the building did not have a vital role to play in the developed cult.

The other small temples in the sanctuary, to Artemis and Aphrodite, are not of great moment in the architectural arrangement, though their presence is interesting from the point of view of the cult. More important are the *abaton* to the north of the temple and the great courtyard building to the south.

The abaton was the building in which the sick passed the night so as to be visited and cured by Asklepios. It lies immediately by the north side of the temple, with only a narrow passage between—appropriately, if the god may be supposed to have come from his temple to visit the sick. Structurally it continues an earlier building of the fifth century identified as a place for bathing, for purification before the ritual. This was supplied by a well, subsequently incorporated inside the abaton. The abaton is essentially a stoa, 118 feet (36 metres) in length (in the Roman period, it was doubled in length by a western extension). The colonnade was in the Ionic order, facing the temple and the area in front of the thymele, and had an upper storey. It was probably built at the same time as the temple. Its proximity to the temple means that it may have overshadowed it somewhat, particularly with its double-storey arrangement. Cult needs, and perhaps the existence of the slope to the north, prevail over sensible planning.

The courtyard building to the south has been regarded as the latest of the principal sanctuary buildings, chiefly on the strength of the architectural details of its porch. I have argued elsewhere that the porch may be a later embellishment of the original structure,[32] and that the main building (that is, the courtyard and the rooms round it) belongs to the fourth-century development. The reason for this is that it appears to fulfil a function essential to the ritual of Asklepios, and that comparable buildings exist at the outset in other sanctuaries of the god; there is no strictly archaeological evidence for this earlier dating. The overall dimensions of the building are 247 feet 9 inches by 228 feet (75·51 by 69·53 metres), excluding the projecting porch and its ramp. The columns of the courtyard number sixteen on each side, and are Doric. The walls have stone footings surmounted by upright slabs (orthostats); but above this they were of unbaked mud brick. Around the courtyard are a variety of rooms, ranging from the long hall on the south side, 42 feet 3 inches by 177 feet 6 inches (12·85 by 54·085 metres), divided by an internal row of columns, through smaller halls on the east and west sides down to small rooms 20 feet 8 inches (6·30 metres) square with off-centre doors in the south-east and south-west corners. The dimensions and arrangement of the doors of these rooms prove that they served as dining-rooms, each with eleven couches; and the remains of couches in the east and south halls (that on the west is less well preserved) show that these were also permanently filled with couches for dining purposes (plate 35).

It seems possible that the courtyard was used for some form of dramatic performance (of a religious and ritual rather than a theatrical character); it was altered to accommodate these more easily in the Roman period, when a small theatre-like structure was actually built in the court. The elaborate porch seems out of character

with the relatively simple architecture of the rest of the building. It is this, together
with the curious way in which it stands clear of the main structure, that makes it
likely to be an afterthought. It consists of a platform 59 feet 4½ inches by 35 feet
10 inches (18·12 by 10·91 metres), linked to the main building by a narrower section
35 feet 8 inches (10·87 metres) wide and 10 feet 10 inches (3·32 metres) deep. On the
front platform, which was approached by a ramp, was a façade of six Doric columns;
on either side, a further three. The linking section carried walls; there were two
columns between them, either Ionic or Corinthian.

This abnormal porch brings with it echoes of the main propylon, and is possibly
similar in date (G. Roux dates the propylon to the early third century).[33] The propylon
has front and rear colonnades of six Doric columns, separated by the long side walls
of the structure and approached by ramps. The abnormality lies in the internal
arrangement. Instead of the normal cross-wall there is an uninterrupted passage
through the structure. In place of the wall there are two internal Corinthian colonnades, each of four columns, behind the front and rear porches and in line with
pilasters on the inside of the side walls. These colonnades are in turn linked by two
sets of two more Corinthian columns, behind the first and fourth of the columns. It is
quite clear that this gateway was designed to impress, to mark formally the entrance
to the sanctuary, rather than to function as a barrier. Indeed, no real barrier was
possible, for Pausanias tells us that the boundary of the sanctuary was defined by
marker stones not by a continuous wall.

The other buildings in the heart of the sanctuary are not of great importance, and
the function of some of them (particularly one adjacent to the south courtyard
building) not properly understood. Pausanias mentions an imposing fountain house,
but this has not been successfully identified. The important structures apart from those
already described are the stadium, which lies in a hollow to the south of the thymele
and is interesting chiefly for its vaulted entrance passage under its north side, clearly
of Hellenistic date (plate 36); the *katagogeion*, a building providing sleeping and eating
accommodation, square in plan, divided into four courtyards each with rooms on all
four sides, and four separate entrances; and, of course, the splendid theatre, constructed
at some distance from the rest of the sanctuary (though still essentially part of it) in
order to take advantage of the hillside to support the great arc of seats (plate 37). The
date of the *katagogeion* is uncertain; the theatre is supposedly of the mid-fourth
century, but as this would put it in the period when building is likely to have been
restricted by financial difficulties, a later date, towards the end of the fourth century—
or, as has recently been suggested on archaeological grounds, the early third century
BC—is more likely.[34]

The sanctuary of Asklepios has distinctive features, and some prominence is given
to certain buildings which would not have received the same treatment in more
conventional sanctuaries. It is remarkable in that it developed at a late date, when
religious patterns were established, and at a time when Greek architects and philo-
sophers were concerned with the proper and rational planning of cities. Yet the factors
which determined the arrangement of the sanctuary are clear. Tradition is foremost
among them; the previous religious usage of the locality, and the sacred places which
had resulted from this; the traditional pattern of temple and altar, and so forth.
Secondly came the particular religious needs of the cult. Having established the

religious site, its development is determined by the requirements and convenience of the ritual and other processes involved. Thirdly, the natural geography of the site, its slopes, hollows and hillsides, the streams and the flat zones have to be taken into consideration. Aesthetic considerations, the architectural concept of the design, lag behind, a poor fourth. Abstract planning, the mindless imposition of a preconceived and rigid design, is totally absent; rather we have a series of areas, pauses on the line of movement through the sanctuary as it were, where some internal coherence is achieved. In this respect, the sanctuary of Asklepios is very much part of the normal pattern of Greek religious usage.

7   Lesser sanctuaries

Aigina, the sanctuary of Aphaia

Aigina affords an excellent example of a middle-sized Greek city-state, the extent of
its territory being clearly defined by the obvious fact that it occupied the whole of the
island in which it is situated. It prospered particularly during the seventh and sixth
centuries, participating in overseas trading adventures, and was one of the mainland
Greek cities to develop close contacts with Egypt during that period. It had a long-
standing hostile relationship with its northern neighbour Athens; this survived into
the fifth century when the development of Athenian power destroyed the former
balance which had existed between them. The urban centre of the state was on the
western side of the island, where the modern town is situated. Not surprisingly, it is
mostly obliterated, leaving only a few tombs of Hellenistic date visible in the outlying parts of the modern town, and the remains of what presumably was the major
sanctuary of the town, that of Apollo, mostly destroyed in the nineteenth century
when its stones were taken to be used in the construction of the harbour.[1]

Outside the town are two other sanctuaries. That of Zeus is remote, on a high pass
near the summit of the island's principal mountain. It is of Hellenistic date, and comprises a terraced area, with a formal stepped approach. At present, it supports a small
Christian church; the precise original arrangement is uncertain.[2] On a lower hillside,
overlooking the north-east corner of the island and the Saronic gulf, is the sanctuary
of Aphaia, a goddess of purely local significance. Her sanctuary was obviously of
considerable importance to the Aiginetans and had achieved monumental form by
the sixth century BC. It was enlarged, and a substantial peripteral Doric temple was
built at the beginning of the fifth century, while Aigina was still rich and prosperous.
With the subsequent decline of the island, it is not surprising that this temple remained,
with only minor alterations.

The sanctuary is situated at the top of a slight rise, along a ridge that runs towards
the north-east and the corner of the island.[3] The sanctuary area is clearly defined by a
continuous boundary, a terrace support wall which forms a substantial level platform
264 feet by 141 feet 1 inch (80·5 by 43 metres). The artificial character of this platform
is emphasized by its regular shape.

Mycenaean objects, discovered during the nineteenth-century excavations, were
taken by the excavators as evidence of a Bronze Age cult, beginning in the fourteenth
century BC. Nothing structural was found, but the material included terracotta
figurines in addition to the inevitable pottery. The site is unlikely to have been a
settlement, at least not one of sufficient importance to produce objects of this type, nor
would it have been a cemetery. The assumption that it was a place of cult, borne out
also by the character of the terracottas, which mostly represent females—perhaps
Aphaia herself—is eminently acceptable. On the other hand, there is no evidence that
proves continuity of cult, however reasonable it may appear to be to assume that

there was. The next sequence of datable objects, mostly pottery, belongs to the eighth century BC and later. They include miniature vessels of a type commonly dedicated in sanctuaries, and prove the existence of cult at that date.

The earliest structures consist of walls delimiting the sanctuary and supporting a terrace fill; and a set of ancillary buildings, together with an altar. Similarity of building material and techniques suggest that they all belong to the same period, earlier than the construction of the sixth-century temple, but almost certainly later than the earliest post-Bronze Age pottery. There are no traces of an early temple of comparable date, but, if there was such a temple, its remains are undoubtedly concealed under the substantial platform of the fifth-century building.

The ancillary buildings seem to have been situated just outside the sanctuary boundary, on the south side, at the south-east corner, and their north wall appears to have served as the boundary in that section. There was in all probability a gateway (rather than a formal propylon building) into the sanctuary immediately to the west. One of the rooms had a raised platform along two at least of its walls, and thus probably served as a dining-room. The purpose of the other rooms is uncertain.

The subsequent sequence of development is complex. Aigina is close to Corinth, and is likely to have been influenced by the seventh-century architectural developments there and at Isthmia. There may well have been a stone temple to Aphaia of the seventh century. The temple at Isthmia, though old-fashioned, seems to have survived into the fifth century, and was not then replaced simply because of its antique character. So the construction of a temple to Aphaia in the sixth century may indicate that the predecessor was not a stone-built temple; or that it had been destroyed accidentally. Our uncertainty compared with Isthmia results partly from the better preserved character of the later temple, and the fact that the investigations at the sanctuary at Aigina were carried out in the nineteenth century, when excavation techniques were less adequate. Of the sixth-century temple several fragments and a possible section of foundation were found. The architectural pieces which survive include column shafts, capitals, parts of the entablature and the roof. The entablature fragments retained distinctly their painted decoration; they also bore traces of fire, clear evidence not only that the temple was short-lived, but that it suffered violent destruction whether by accident or a deliberate act of hostility. The nineteenth-century excavators dated this second temple to the first third of the sixth century BC, partly on the comparison of its architectural forms with those of the archaic temple on the Athenian Acropolis, partly because of the pottery discovered under the foundations. A date about 570 seems consistent with its flat, saucer-shaped Doric capitals, and is confirmed by recent excavations.[4] These have revealed that the temple was peripteral, despite the fact that the original excavators reconstructed a narrow non-peripteral building, its porch containing two Doric columns, and its cella the unusual arrangement of two inner rooms side by side at its end. Even this is dubious, based on the analogy of what was once thought to be the original form of the archaic temple at Athens. The existence of long, narrow, non-peripteral temples elsewhere in the adjacent mainland region (the temple at Porto Cheli, now under water, recently discovered by the Americans)[5] suggests that the Athenian analogy is unnecessary, and the two inner rooms did not exist.

The reconstructed temple would seem at first to have made use of the original altar; this suggests that it was on the same alignment as the first temple and, in all probability, directly overlying it. About the middle of the sixth century an improvement of the eastern end to the sanctuary was carried out. This was recorded on an inscription, which refers to the building of a house, and altar, and a precinct wall. The wall was constructed on the slope that leads down to the east. After a short section which links it to the original north wall, a long straight section runs in a southeasterly direction, past the ancillary building of the earlier sanctuary. A larger area was thus made available to the east of the temple, and on this, east of its original position but on a similar alignment, was constructed a more massive altar, parts of whose foundations remain. The excavators believed that this period of construction also involved the addition of a portico to the north of the ancillary building, together with a more monumental propylon to its west. The German scholar G. Welter, on the basis of construction methods, supposes a more radical reconstruction in this area, with the building of a westward return at the southern end of the new eastern precinct wall up to and including a more massive propylon, which continued to serve the sanctuary at the time of the third temple, built after the fire had destroyed the second. This theory has been more recently rejected by Miss Bergquist.[6]

The destruction of the second temple led to the final reorganization of the sanctuary. There was a further enlargement of the sanctuary area, with new substantial support walls to north, east, and south, assuming that this was not reconstructed already at the middle of the sixth century. North and south walls were now parallel to each other; the west wall at right angles to them and only the surviving east wall at a different angle to prevent the conformation of the sanctuary to a rigidly rectangular form. The new temple was larger than the earlier and, at last, on a new alignment, with its sides parallel to the terrace support walls. This new temple conformed to the standard peripteral type of Doric structure, with six columns across the façade, though only twelve instead of the more usual thirteen along the flanks (fig. 18). In front was a new, more massive altar, centred on the axis of the temple in strict alignment (plate 38). Flanking the altar were bases for a series of statues, probably of young maidens. Outside the propylon was a separate terrace, closed on the east side by the ancillary buildings now, if not earlier, in their most elaborate form, while on the south side there was a wall, perhaps with its own propylon. At some distance from the sanctuary, to south and west, were isolated buildings, perhaps houses or entertainment rooms. At some distance down the slope to the north-east of the sanctuary there are the remains of a fountain house at a natural spring.

This final reconstruction belongs to the years around 500 BC. There were subsequently some renewals and other modifications made to the temple, but in the years after the defeat of the Persians (in which the Aiginetan fleet had played a substantial and valiant part) the decline of Aigina's power and wealth made any further redevelopment impossible. The sanctuary remained a perfect example of the transitional period between the archaic and fifth-century classical. The excavators report finds of pottery dating to Hellenistic times; the absence of Roman pottery in the report may reflect the attitudes of nineteenth-century archaeologists to such material rather than its total absence, but they do state that a lamp of the first century AD was the only object of later times found. Pausanias mentions the sanctuary, but says nothing about it, beyond the legend and explanation that on Aigina Aphaia is a title of the

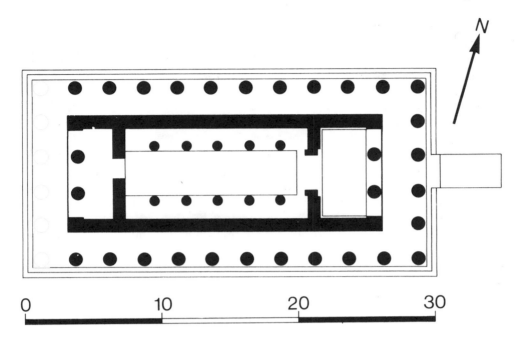

18 The temple of Aphaia, Aigina: plan

goddess Artemis. At all events, it is clear that Aphaia was one of many sanctuaries in mainland Greece which did not receive any significant support during the Roman period.

The sanctuary of Aphaia displays several interesting features, which call for some comment. That the rise and subsequent stagnation of the sanctuary reflect the history of the state in which it was situated is understandable, but it also emphasizes the dependence of the sanctuary on the local community. From the archaeological point of view, the sanctuary is important because of the relative clarity with which the successive phases of development can be seen, even if there are points of obscurity and uncertainty, particularly with regard to the exact form of the two earlier temple buildings. Here it is worth remarking on the early establishment of the essential elements in the sanctuary; temple, altar, precinct wall with its entrance and the adjacent ancillary structures. All these reflect a continuing ritual need achieved in an increasingly monumental form as the sanctuary developed. Though the elements remain constant, the gradual rearrangement of them is interesting. The earliest sanctuary (disregarding the probable original, totally undeveloped and unmonumental form) was irregular in shape, keeping close to the natural contours of the site, so as not to overtax the skill of the builders or to make the wall too massive. All the elements were in scale, but the only monumentality was, presumably, the assumed alignment between temple and altar. The second phase begins with a more substantial temple, but continues by extending the sanctuary also to a more monumental form, with the new terrace wall nearly parallel to the façade of the temple. These tendencies are then developed most fully in the final arrangement, which incorporates the most monumental forms for the individual buildings, and relates more rigidly the temple and altar to the symmetry of the sanctuary. Such symmetry is more typical of the sanctuaries in the east Greek area, and it is possible that the Aiginetans, who were in close contact with the east Greek cities, sharing with them the establishment of Naukratis in Egypt, may have been inspired from that direction; though its most perfect achievement belongs to a time when the east Greeks were under the domination of Persia, and the enterprise of Naukratis in decline. It is therefore better to regard this quality of symmetry as something that developed of its own accord at Aigina, the progress to which is to be seen in the successive building stages of this sanctuary.

The sanctuary was not particularly well endowed with statuary other than that of the third temple; the prepared and carefully aligned bases flanking the altar have been noted. Several fragments were taken to Munich in the early nineteenth century, along with the temple sculpture, and other pieces were found by the excavators; but there is no general scattering of bases, and the contrast between the quantity of temple sculpture and other sculpture preserved is noticeable. On the whole, it seems that the sanctuary was not cluttered up with monuments, perhaps because its importance faded in the fifth century when the adornment of sanctuaries with sculpture was gathering force.

Nemea

The Nemean games were celebrated originally at the sanctuary of Zeus near the modern village of Heraklion, a little to the west of the main road from Corinth to Argos, at the head of a valley which drops northwards down to the Corinthian gulf. It is thus separated, by easy mountain passes, from the territory of Kleonai to the east, Argos to the south and Phleious to the west; but when the games were developed, apparently in the sixth century BC, it would seem that the district was under the control of Kleonai. Kleonai, however, enjoyed a close relationship with Argos, and the games were generally under Argive control. Eventually their celebration was transferred to Argos itself.[7]

The site is the one where, according to legend, Herakles wrestled with the Nemean Lion, and it probably achieved an early sanctity. The valley was inhabited in the Bronze Age and later, but in classical times cannot have contained more than villages; the sanctuary is essentially a rural one. It is dominated at the present day by the remains of the fourth-century temple, three columns of which are still standing, surrounded by much of the remainder, overthrown by an earthquake, perhaps in the fourth century AD. Sporadic excavations have been carried out, by the French and, more recently, the Americans, who are now conducting the thorough investigation needed so that the sanctuary and its history can be fully elucidated. There are traces of an earlier temple, of the sixth century BC, and presumably belonging to the time when the games were first being developed.

The later arrangements are more clearly visible, and easier to study.[8] The fourth-century temple lies over the earlier building, but not on the same axis (plate 39). It is a Doric structure, of the shortened fourth-century type, 65 feet 7 inches by 139 feet 7 inches (20 by 42·55 metres), with six columns across the façade and only twelve along the side. There is the usual front porch, but no false porch at the rear. The cella contains an inner colonnade of Corinthian columns; at the back of the cella behind the colonnade is a crypt, taking the place of the false porch, its floor apparently at the ground level of the original temple. In front of the temple is a long altar, not axially aligned with it; its position may reflect rather the position of the earlier temple. A ramp leads up to the temple platform from behind the altar; it is apparently a later addition.

To the south of the temple, some 235 feet (72 metres) away at its nearest point is a range of ancillary buildings, excavated by the Americans but not yet published. Their alignment is slightly different from that of the temple. They are of much cheaper construction, unbaked brick with timber ties over stone footings (orthostats). They would appear to consist of guest-rooms, presumably for the more distinguished visitors to the festival (similar rooms being provided at other important rural sanc-tuaries). A separate section, with stone tubs round the wall and a water channel feeding them through lion's-head spouts, provided washing facilities. A short distance to the south-east, on higher hillsides above the valley floor, is the site of the former stadium, now a vineyard, producing the sweet black grapes for which the region is famous. Though only a very small part has recently been excavated, the shape of the stadium is clearly discernible.

The second temple has been dated by the Americans to the years between 340 and 320 BC. The ancillary buildings are later (at one point they are constructed over a kiln used to fire the terracotta tiles of the temple, and subsequently filled in), but know-ledge of their exact chronology awaits publication by the American excavators. It seems reasonable to suppose that there were more buildings and monuments in the sanctuary, at present unknown. Unknown also are the exact limits of the sacred area. The Americans consider that the ancillary buildings are along the southern border of the sacred area. If the stadium was within them, the area must have been extensive, but the analogy of Isthmia, where the stadium is some distance from the sanctuary, suggests that it was outside. Equally, it is possible that there was an earlier stadium in the sanctuary itself.

The chronology of the later temple points to a redevelopment of a sixth-century sanctuary which had perhaps suffered from the wars and invasions that afflicted this area in the fourth century BC. Such redevelopment presupposes a return to more stable conditions, and a desire to repair earlier damage; this points to the years imme-diately following the battle of Chaironeia in 338, and the peace settlement imposed on the Greek cities by the Macedonian king, Philip II. The Macedonian kings claimed descent from the old royal family of Argos (one of whom was in exile at Kleonai in the sixth century, and thus may be associated with the earlier development of the sanctuary). Argos was politically favoured by the Macedonians, and the restoration of sanctuaries would have been encouraged by them. The temple itself, as the Ameri-cans have shown, is conservative and Peloponnesian in character, the work surely of a local architect; and its lack of embellishment, with the apparent failure to execute the intended pediment sculpture, together with the simple construction of the ancillary structures, suggests that it received no great financial aid from the Mace-donians, but, rather, was dependent on Argive funds.

The further history of the sanctuary is equally obscure. After the celebration of the games had been evacuated to Argos, Aratos of Sikyon made an attempt in 235 BC to revive them at Nemea as an act of political purpose in the struggle between the

Achaean league, of which he was general, and the tyrants of Argos, but this is unlikely to have outlasted the union of Argos with the league. By the second century AD the temple was roofless and the cult-statue gone.[9]

Brauron

The sanctuary of Artemis at Brauron is situated on the east coast of Attica behind Mounts Pentelicus and Hymettus, a region which was incorporated with the Athenian state long before the historical period, although it retained local traditions, its local ruling families, and its local cults.[10] The cult was important enough to be established also on the Acropolis at Athens, indicating not only the total assimilation of the area into the Athenian state, but probably the emergence of its leading families in the political life of the wider state. The two cults were linked, and at the rural festival a procession made its way from the sanctuary on the Acropolis to Brauron. One of the features of the cult was that young girls selected from leading Athenian families served as priestesses for a period before marriage. As priestesses, they were known as 'bears', an indication of the connection of the Artemis cult with wildlife.

The earliest archaeological evidence from the area of the sanctuary suggests that it did not begin to develop until the seventh century BC. Even so, no traces of building from that period have been identified, and the cult centred on a natural cave connected with the burial place of the legendary first priestess of Artemis, Iphigeneia, daughter of Agamemnon and Clytemnestra. This cave is situated on the northern lower slopes of a hill; there are foundations of buildings round it. To the north-west of this, but still on the slopes of the hill, stood the temple, a Doric temple of the late sixth or early fifth century BC. Of this, only the foundations remain. It was not a large building, measuring about twenty metres in length by about eleven in width. Like most temples of Artemis, it faced west, and the altar was situated on this side, though not directly in front of the temple.

Architecturally, the sanctuary is most interesting for its ancillary buildings; these lie mostly to the north and east of the temple, on low ground which is now marshy and often flooded. A road approached from the west, presumably that along which the procession from Athens made its way. It led into the sanctuary over a bridge, an interesting structure of slabs resting on piers, and wide enough (about ten metres) to take several people or animals side by side. Next to this came the outer wall of a stoa, a three-sided structure round a court, at the fourth side of which (the south) was the tomb of Iphigeneia. The sides are of unequal length; that on the west had to stop short against the temple platform in a most awkward arrangement. The east side reached further towards the hill slope. Only the north colonnade was completed, those to east and west having nothing more than foundations apart from the first column next to the corner. The entrance lay through the middle of the west side, with openings to front and back and a cross-wall between with two doorways— rather like an enclosed propylon. There were rooms to either side, entered from the colonnade of the court. On the north side was a set of six square rooms, with one smaller room at the end, and a passageway in the middle giving access to another open colonnade, facing north. The main rooms on this side contained stone tables, and the positions were clearly marked for couches round the walls, three on each side, except for the position by the door. Three of the rooms on the west side were also arranged with off-centre doors to hold the standard eleven couches.

On the assumption that the little bear-priestesses lived away from their parents and in the sanctuary during their term of office, it has been argued that this building was the one in which they lived. The striking similarity between the rooms equipped for couches and the formal dining-rooms of other sanctuaries suggests rather that they served this function here also. Inscriptions found in the sanctuary have been interpreted as indicating that this building was known as the Parthenon, the building of the Virgin, but a recent study denies this, suggesting instead that the name was given rather to the temple itself. The inscriptions indicate that the colonnade was built in 416 BC. It overlies the remains of older structures, not fully elucidated, which may well be earlier versions of this building, serving the same functions.

The other approach to the sanctuary was from the east, that is, from the sea. This roadway passed to the north of the portico building, along the side of its outer wall. On the opposite side of the road at this point was another very shallow portico, of wooden posts rather than columns. This was exactly the same length as the main north portico, and the section of roadway between the two was closed at either end by double doorways. It has been suggested that this narrow portico served as a place of dedication, where the clothes of women who had died in childbirth were given to Artemis.

Perachora

The sanctuary of Hera at Perachora (the place-name is that of the modern village) was of no great importance. It received only incidental mention in the ancient literature—a bald reference by the geographer Strabo, and a little more information by Xenophon, about the occasion when the locality was the scene of Spartan military activity early in the fourth century BC.[11] There are no significant inscriptions from the site, apart from the record of the goddess's name which permits the sanctuary's identification. No famous visitors came there, it attracted no notable gifts from the great men in history—or at least, none that was recorded, for, as we shall see, there is a possibility that one of the Hellenistic kings did interest himself in it. Its importance depends on our archaeological knowledge; and though the individual buildings in it are not particularly well preserved, they have been thoroughly investigated, and together they present an interesting picture of the development and functioning of the sanctuary, its improvement at the end of the fourth century BC, and its decline.[12]

The sanctuary is situated almost at the end of the long promontory running westwards into the Gulf of Corinth, dividing the innermost recesses of that gulf into a southern part, which ends at Corinth town and the Isthmus of Corinth, and a northern, which gives some access to the forbidding south coast of Boeotia. The promontory ends with a cape, dangerous to shipping and at present marked by a lighthouse. Otherwise the nearest permanent habitation (there is much unfortunate development of holiday villas and bungalows for summer occupation) is at Perachora village, some six miles to the east. Below the lighthouse, under the southern cliffs, is a small cove with a beach, exposed to all but the northerly winds; in calm weather it does provide a possible landing place for small boats. The sanctuary begins on a low ledge behind the beach, but still below the cliffs; this is in fact the lower end of a small enclosed valley which rises, steep-sided, towards the east until finally enclosed by a pointed hill, the end of the ridge forming the backbone of the promontory. It was not long before the area of religious use extended into this valley; and it is possible that the whole of it was sacred land, distinct from the sanctuary in the strict sense, but still excluded from normal, secular use. Strabo says that the sanctuary was that of an oracle, but there is no conclusive archaeological evidence to support this.

The earliest evidence for the development of the sanctuary comprises fragments of pottery, of the ninth century BC. There are no traces of Bronze Age occupation. The earliest building had its footings sunk into the levels which contained these fragments of pottery, and is likely therefore to be a little later in date—possibly as late as the middle of the eighth century.[13] The footings alone are partly preserved. It was a small, apsidal building, 25 feet by 18 feet (7·62 by 5·49 metres), with walls of unbaked brick and a thatched roof supported on wooden posts. It is not likely to have had a long life. Its appearance is perhaps best judged by terracotta models, deposited in the sanctuary as offerings to the goddess, and quite clearly intended to represent her temple. The walls of these models have meander patterns painted on them, possibly reflecting the way in which real walls were decorated (a concept that seems to have survived as late as the first monumental temples in stone, such as that of Poseidon at Isthmia). The shape of the roof on these models and the way the painted decoration is applied clearly indicate that the original was thatch, and, indeed, no tile fragments were found in the ruins.

Some time after this, probably after the end of the eighth century BC, another building identified as a temple was constructed away from the beach, higher up in the valley. This was rectangular and contained a hearth (or altar). The superstructure was still of mud brick, but the stones of the footing were more carefully selected and trimmed to fit each other. Inscriptions on vases and a bronze statuette indicate a dedication to Hera Limenia, Hera of the Harbour, and the cult under this epithet was distinguished by the original excavators from that of the lower temple, dedicated to Hera Akraia, Hera of the Headland. This is rather dubious. It has been seriously doubted that there ever was a special category of temple with internal hearth altars (see below, the discussion of the Sanctuary of Herakles on Thasos). Though the lower temple was reconstructed in the sixth century, this other building was not, though there was much later work carried out in the vicinity. The original building cannot have had a very long life, and, if this is so, the 'separate' cult of Hera Limenia was short lived. It seems best to regard Akraia and Limenia as descriptive epithets for a single cult, centred on the temple and altar by the little harbour. The higher ground behind was reserved for ancillary and other structures, of which the 'temple of Hera Limenia' (perhaps in reality a dining-room) was one. Other archaic elements in the functioning of the sanctuary in this ancillary area included an artificial pool; when excavated, this was found to contain several bronze bowls, and it was suggested that this was in some way connected with the operation of the sanctuary as an oracle. There is no proof of this.

The sanctuary flourished in the seventh and sixth centuries BC during the great period of Corinth's prosperity. Considerable quantities of offerings, metalwork and pottery were deposited. This demonstrates that, by this time, the sanctuary served more than the local communities of the Perachora promontory, which were never large or wealthy enough to make offerings on this scale. Clearly, the majority of the worshippers came from Corinth town, only a short distance by sea across the gulf; Perachora had been Corinthian territory, probably since the mid-eighth century, the time when the sanctuary begins to develop from its simple origins. There is no reason to suppose that the sanctuary was exclusively Corinthian; the region had connections of some sort with the neighbouring Megarian communities, possibly more than geographical, and it was equally accessible for the next of the independent cities along the Gulf of Corinth, namely Sikyon (Sikyonian coins have been found in the neighbourhood of the sanctuary).[14]

In the sixth century there was considerable development. Massive terrace walls were built for the upper part (though not, apparently, any buildings). In the lower sanctuary as substantial a temple was constructed, in the Doric order, as the restrictions of the site between cliff and sea would allow. This was placed to the west of the old temple and facing a wide altar of the type decorated with triglyph and metope panels favoured in Corinth and the Argolid. Further round an extended open space was formed by cutting away part of the rock; it would seem that it was expected that worshippers would come to the sanctuary in increasing numbers. The journey to Perachora from Corinth, even by sea, would take some time, and it is clear that the worshippers were likely to need to spend at least a night in the vicinity of the sanctuary. There was no village near enough to provide accommodation, and instead it would appear that the worshippers camped out in the fields above the sanctuary and the valley in which it was situated.[15] Here there are also the remains of simple houses which could have been used for this purpose (significantly, one of the earlier ones is equipped with a special dining-room for feasts) and another, small temple, of unknown cult.[16]

Despite the sixth-century development, the sanctuary appears to have passed the peak of its success in the fifth century. Offerings are reduced, both in number and quality. There are several possible explanations of this. Corinth was not so prosperous in the face of Athenian economic development, and people would not have so much to offer. The reduction in the quantity of offerings is attested for the fifth century in other sanctuaries, not just those of Corinth. There is the possibility that there were substantial offerings of greater individual intrinsic value, and that these, unlike the earlier gifts, were not buried on the site but robbed and lost. Even so, the sanctuary experienced no architectural development in the fifth or fourth century (until its closing years) and the impression of decline is almost certainly the most accurate one. The buildings were adequate for their purpose, and failing accidental damage (the Spartan attack was not directed at the sanctuary or its religious administration) there was no call for further development.

Nothing more was done, then, until the end of the fourth century. The temple did not need rebuilding. In the lower part of the sanctuary the courtyard area was enlarged considerably by cutting away the shelly rock (a natural marine deposit) and lining it with stone blocks. There was a low bench in front of this wall. To the east of the temple and altar a two-storey stoa was constructed, shutting off the lower sanctuary from the valley and the upper part.[17] There were no rooms behind the colonnade (there was not the space for them); the lower storey was Doric, the upper

Ionic. On the ground floor there was, again, a low bench round the wall. The building is dated principally by the architectural forms employed; the courtyard extension, on the other hand, is dated by the pottery found in the space between the rock cutting and the facing wall added in front of it. The lower sanctuary, though still desperately restricted in size, could now accommodate as large a group of worshippers as possible.

The upper area did not receive the same development; there are no traces of fourth-century buildings, though by now the terrace wall construction had obliterated the 'sacred pool'. This is strange, for there are not the same limitations in space, but only if the upper area is regarded as a distinct sanctuary. If (as is argued above) it is not, then the reason for concentrating development round the harbour is obvious. In the upper area development is restricted to the region below the lowest of the terrace walls. Here was built a double set of dining-rooms, each room accommodating eleven stone couches of standard dimensions (presumably padded mattresses were used with them) still partly preserved. The dimensions are the same as those of dining-rooms found elsewhere, the nearest examples being those in the sanctuary of Asklepios at Corinth. The rooms were substantially built, the surviving parts of the wall formed from large but irregular blocks of stone, while the floors are of pebble cement, with a raised plaster band under the couches. In front, and obviously part of the same construction since it is precisely aligned with the dining-rooms, is a large storage tank which collected, through a substantial drainage system, the surface rain-water that fell in the upper area (plate 40). A settling tank ensured that the water was filtered before it was stored. It is possible that this tank replaced the 'sacred pool'; but may have contained drinking water, which could also be used for purification purposes. The tank is an unusual construction. It was excavated into the ground (mostly loose rubble washed down from the higher parts of the valley) and lined with large blocks of regular ashlar masonry. The floor was cement over rubble, and the cement was extended up the sides to give complete waterproofing. The roof was probably wooden—nothing of it survives—and rested on an inner line of stone piers. Some of these, where the tank was sunk more deeply into the sloping floor of the valley, also supported horizontal stone beams to prevent the side walls bulging in under the pressure of the unstable material against which they were built. There was also a most ingenious, cantilevered stone stairway leading into the tank, and a drainage pipe ran off down to the sanctuary (which it possibly supplied with water, though no trace of the receiving end has survived).

This was not the only new work carried out. In the region above the valley and the sanctuary a serious attempt was made to improve the amenities for the worshippers who came to the festivals.[18] New houses were built, again with dining-rooms for feasting provided in them. In addition, a most elaborate scheme was devised to provide this area also with abundant water supplies—water, in fact, seems to have been the most serious problem for this sanctuary. There were no natural springs which could be tapped or streams which could be diverted and stored. The only source of water (apart from rain, assiduously collected in the sanctuary) lay a hundred feet underground. To reach this, three shafts of wide rectangular section were dug together with an approach staircase and connecting tunnels. It was intended that water should be lifted by means of these shafts (probably by an endless chain of buckets turning over a wheel) and fed into a supply channel, buried underground and sealed with tiles and plaster. This led to three storage tanks, again underground, and some distance from the shafts. The rock in front of the tanks was cut away, and a superb Ionic fountain house built, the water being drawn from cement-lined stone basins, one in front of each tank. The system is extremely complex, and would require machinery, perhaps worked by animals, to lift the water. It seems possible that the machinery was not installed, and that therefore the system was never put in working order—a grandiose idea that came to nothing.[19] Thereafter, the sanctuary declined rapidly.

The elaborate works of the late fourth century require explanation. They were carried through at a time when religious building, including general development within the sanctuaries, was unusual. True, after the complete stagnation of the mid-fourth century, the conquests of Alexander and the resources that they released led to a stimulation of activity in the old Greek area; but this was soon followed by depopulation, and a shift in importance to the eastern Mediterranean. Wealthy individuals occasionally made donations to the sanctuaries of the mainland which resulted in building work being undertaken, but it was normally the more prestigious sanctuaries that benefited from this. Perachora was not one of these. Instead, this development would appear to have a political purpose, and to be thus accidental, as far as religious usage was concerned. At the time when these works were carried out (they all belong to the same time, more or less 300 BC), Corinth was under the control of a Macedonian dynast, Demetrius; it was, in fact, about all that was left to him from the vast area formerly controlled by his father, Antigonos the one-eyed, who had been one of the leading contestants for control of Alexander's empire, only to be finally defeated and killed at the battle of Ipsus in 301 BC. Demetrius clung to his now petty kingdom, despite the offence this gave to the Greeks who had been granted their freedom only a few years previously by Antigonos. It seems likely that the elaborate improvements at Perachora were designed to win the favour of the Corinthians, as much as the goddess at whose sanctuary they were carried out. It is known that Demetrius was personally interested in machinery and technology, and the elaborate waterworks system is in keeping with this.[20] Its apparent failure is also entirely in keeping with Demetrius' unhappy and unsuccessful career.

Thasos, the sanctuary of Herakles

The cult of Herakles seems to have been the most important one in the city of Thasos.[21] Herakles appears on Thasian coinage, and he has the title, among others, of protector of the city. The origin of the cult is obscure, for Herakles' own status was somewhat confusing. It was recognized that, as the son of Zeus and the mortal Alkmena, he was a human, a hero rather than a god; but also that he subsequently attained divine status. The question affects the nature of the ritual which was offered to him, but on Thasos there can be no doubt that he was worshipped as a god and that his sanctuary was organized accordingly, though probably arranged so that it could accommodate the 'offerings to the dead'—made by making sacrifices at a pit rather than at an altar—which were appropriate to a hero. The sanctuary is situated within the fortified area of the city (fig. 19).

Despite Herakles' importance to the city and despite the wealth of Thasos, at least

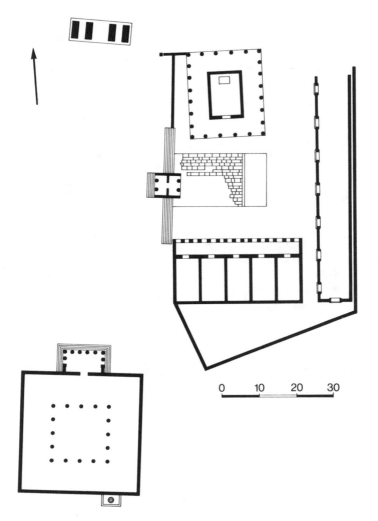

19 The sanctuary of Herakles, Thasos

in the early period (the island possessed gold mines on the opposite mainland, though she lost these to Athens in the fifth century and to Macedon in the fourth), the sanctuary is a surprisingly modest one. According to the latest elucidation of its chronology, it was first organized in the early seventh century BC, shortly after the first arrival of Greek colonists from the Cycladic island of Paros. The early sanctuary was extremely simple, consisting only of a primitive altar, a roughly rectangular mass of native rock trimmed at the sides. It is not clear whether it was given a masonry casing at this early date; probably not. This was for the normal burnt sacrifices to Herakles as a god. By this there were small pits, probably to receive the offerings to the cult of Herakles as a hero. At this stage there is no other trace of any organization in the sanctuary. Its boundaries and entrance are undefined (though probably the same as those which can be recognized at a later date) and there was no temple.

The first significant architectural development did not come until the mid-sixth century, and even then is still very simple. A short distance to the south-west of the altar area a rectangular building was constructed with a porch facing north, that is, to the front of the altar. There was a single supporting post to the porch between the side walls. A door in the rear wall of the porch led to the main room, in the rear wall of which another door gave access to a very small back chamber. This is not a large building; it is only about 20 feet 8 inches (6·3 metres) wide internally, and the main room has a length of about 37 feet 1 inch (11·3 metres). In the centre of this room is a hearth, and two more posts to support the roof. The original publication of this building by its excavators naturally assumed that it was the temple, and that the hearth served as an altar. However, Birgitta Bergquist in her recent study of the sanctuary has noted that the width of 20 feet 8 inches is similar to that of formal dining-rooms, and has suggested, plausibly, that this Thasian building served the same function, the hearth, as in the other dining-rooms, being principally for heating. Such an arrangement would require the doors to be off-centre but this cannot be proved (or, of course, disproved, by the badly preserved remains). If this argument is accepted, it is interesting that such a building took precedence over a temple. The temple was not constructed until the first half of the fifth century. It is possible that an earlier, simpler structure was then superseded, and did not leave sufficient remains to be noticed by the excavators. It is significant, however, that the first buildings in the sanctuary of Apollo on Delos (very close to the original home of the inhabitants of Thasos, the island of Paros) were not temples. The most important early building is the so-called 'oikos of the Naxians'. The population of the Aegean islands was the least disturbed by the upheavals of the end of the late Bronze Age, and so most likely to retain older religious traditions, which did not require temples in the sanctuaries.

The temple was a small but fully peripteral building. The cella was very simple, no porch, no false porch at the back, merely a rectangular room with a door and the cult-statue at the back. Around this was a broadly spaced Ionic colonnade 65 feet 11 inches by 76 feet 8 inches (20·1 by 23·4 metres), curiously square proportions which again suggest that Thasos was not an area of architectural convention either by the standards of mainland or of east Greece. Also unconventional was the alignment of the temple, which faced due south, towards the altar, perhaps suggesting midday as an important time in the ritual, but possibly implying nothing more than expediency, as the essential arrangements of the sanctuary were already determined—the position of the altar and the entrance—and there was not enough room to place the temple in the conventional way to the west of the altar.

There were other considerable improvements to the sanctuary made at this time or in the subsequent century. The altar, then if not before, was given a masonry casing. The area to the west of the altar was paved. A precinct wall was constructed running close to the west side of the temple, enclosing an angled yard behind the dining-room, and closing in the sanctuary on the east. On the west side (as mentioned earlier) the wall was interrupted, and replaced by the broad flight of steps which seemed to have served as a viewpoint for the games and other activities which took place to the west; at the centre of this was the propylon, a formal entrance rather than a barrier, projecting outwards from the steps, and of the usual H form, with a single door and two columns for each of its porches. Behind the altar was a long narrow room, with doorways at regular intervals facing into the sanctuary, and with an additional door at its south end into the angled court. The function of this building is completely uncertain; the precinct wall ran immediately behind its blank, eastern wall.

On the south side of the sanctuary (and forming the front of the angled court) the dining-room building was reconstructed, using the same outer foundations, and extended by the addition of another four rooms. The simple porch in front of the original room was replaced by an extended portico. The evidence for the doorways into these rooms is scanty, but less so than for the earlier, single room, and, if not conclusive, is not incompatible with an off-centre door. As before, the rooms are 20 feet 8 inches (6·3 metres) wide, and with the use of the standard couch dimension of 6 feet by 2 feet 10 inches (1·80 by 0·85 metres) all five rooms can be restored as dining-rooms, with two couches by the front wall (and the space of a couch occupied by the door), three couches along the back wall, and six couches along the sides, which are 38 feet 5 inches (11·7 metres) long, each wall also accommodating the foot of one couch. The building is thus very similar to the sets of dining-rooms at Perachora, the Athenian Asklepieion and Brauron, the chief difference being in their depth. The western wall of the western room forms the boundary of the precinct. At the other side a narrow passageway between this building and the enigmatic east building leads into the angled court. The only feature observed in this court was a deep pit, full of water. The excavators suggested that it had a ritual purpose, but, given its water-logged character, it is more likely to have been a well. If so, given the identification of the south building as a set of dining-rooms, the angled court is more probably a subordinate, kitchen area than a strict part of the sanctuary (to which it would then form an addition, not an original part).

The final additions to this complex took place outside the demarcated boundary of the sanctuary, and concern the area to the west identified as the area of contests and display (watched from the stepped area). On the south side of this a large courtyard building was constructed at the end of the fourth or beginning of the third century BC. An inscription from its architrave partly preserves the name of Thersilochos, presumably its donor. It has not been adequately published, and the plans show it to be about 33 metres square with a central peristyle 15 metres square (measured on the axis of the columns) but without, apparently, any internal dividing walls. It was approached through a splendid, projecting colonnaded porch, on the top of a flight of steps. This porch recalls that leading to the dining-court at Epidauros, of similar date; and though this Thasian example does not have the same corroborative evidence for the arrangement of its rooms, it is not unlikely that it formed another such building. Alternatively, with its formal porch, it could have been the destination for sacred processions, and perhaps for the performances of a dramatic nature—a purpose which I have postulated for the dining-court at Epidauros. The addition of a well at the south side of this building adds extra weight to its interpretation as a dining-court. If this is accepted, we have at Thasos the strange situation where the architectural arrangements to accommodate the diners quite outshine those of the temple and the other ritual.

Arcadian sanctuaries

Arcadia is the central region of the Peloponnese, highlands divided by considerable mountain ranges. It seems to have provided a place of refuge at the end of the late Bronze Age, and, more clearly than in other regions of Greece, its inhabitants in classical times were the direct descendants of the Bronze Age population.[22] It contained, until the fourth century BC, only two really important cities, both on the central plateau: Tegea to the south and Mantinea to the north. Other places, such as Orchomenos to the west of Mantinea, were of old foundation but not in themselves important places. The only other sizeable city was Megalopolis, an artificial foundation coalescing the populations of several villages created in the 360s to provide a bastion against Sparta (which at last had been seriously defeated in battle) and a centre for a new federal system under which the whole of Arcadia was to be united. Because of its mountainous situation and its isolation from the sea with its benefits of trade, Arcadia was not one of the richest areas of Greece; its principal product might seem to be its young men, who served as mercenary soldiers for other states and commanders, particularly in the fourth century BC.

None of its sanctuaries can be said to have had more than local significance. Few were equipped with really splendid buildings, and few have remained sufficiently well preserved to present a reasonably complete archaeological impression. There are two temples of major importance, that of Apollo at Bassai (plates 41 and 42), a place high in the south-western mountains, belonging to the territory of the small town of Phigaleia, and dated essentially to the second half of the fifth century BC; and that of Athena Alea at Tegea, of the mid-fourth century (plate 43).[23] In addition, there is the sanctuary of a goddess called Despoina (the Mistress) at Lykosoura, in the mountains behind Megalopolis, where most of the structures appear to be of Hellenistic date or later (plate 44).[24] Other sanctuaries have less to tell us. There was an archaic temple at Orchomenos, of which there are some remains.[25] Mantinea's important sanctuary of Poseidon Hippios, Horse Poseidon, is known to have been situated just outside the town but there are no material remains from it.[26] There is a very strange, inadequately understood sanctuary at Lusoi, in northern Arcadia.[27] Only at Lykosoura is it really possible to elucidate the full arrangement of the sanctuary. At Bassai, apart from the well-preserved temple, little remains, though the foundations of its predecessor have been excavated recently.[28] At Tegea, though the temple and foundations of a rectangular altar have been excavated, the rest of the sanctuary has not. Lusoi is badly preserved. None of them, perhaps, deserves full individual treatment, but collectively they demonstrate certain features which are not without interest.

First, the temples themselves do not conform precisely with the established classical types, at Olympia, Athens and elsewhere. Lusoi is the most peculiar, presenting an enigmatic plan of a narrow central hall with a deep porch (with an equally deep false porch at the back), and long narrow rooms to either side, entered through the doors in the sides of the main hall (fig. 20). It is doubtful whether we can place much reliance on the accuracy of this plan, which is a restoration based on structures which were only partly preserved and possibly misunderstood by the excavator. The door in the side wall is certain, and provides a link with the other Arcadian temples, which also have doors in their side walls, as well as the principal door behind the main porch. At

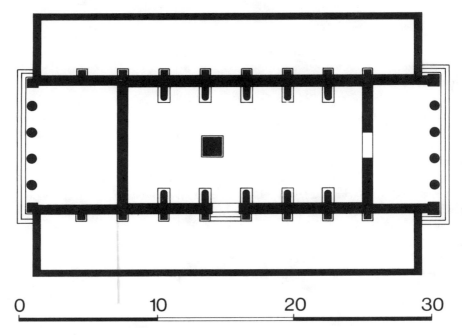

0   10   20   30

20 The temple at Lusoi

Bassai, a peripteral Doric temple built on a north–south alignment rather than the conventional east–west, there is a large door in the east wall, towards the end of the cella, opening into a space behind the internal colonnade. It might be considered that this arrangement results from the awkwardness of the siting in the sanctuary, caused by the mountainous locality; that there was not room to place the temple on the usual east–west alignment, and that the door in the east side is a compromise, to allow the cult-statue to look out to the rising sun. This is difficult to believe, for though the site is a little cramped, it would not have been impossible to build the temple on the more normal alignment, and the discovery of the foundations belonging to an older temple, also on a north–south alignment but smaller in size, supports this; unfortunately, these foundations are not sufficiently well preserved to allow us to determine whether or not there was a door in the east wall. There does appear to have been an inner room (rather than a false porch) at the south end, and it is not impossible that there was a door to this in the east side. The whole temple, which was crudely built with unlevel floors, is long and narrow, about 79 by 25 feet (about 24 by 7·50 metres), a feature which is retained in the fifth-century, peripteral version. Athena Alea at Tegea has a more conventional Doric peripteral temple aligned east–west, but there is a door in the side (north) wall of the cella, with a ramp leading up to the temple platform in front of it. This door is much smaller than the side door at Bassai, and the main door of the temple itself.

The temple at Lykosoura is smaller and non-peripteral. The main door faces approximately towards the east, through a porch of six Doric columns, but again there is a door in the side wall (south) of the cella, with its own steps. The orientation of the side doors at Tegea and Lykosoura clearly demonstrates that they have nothing to do with the sun. (It is interesting that there is another important temple with a door in a side wall, that of Zeus at Nemea, situated in Dorian territory administered by Argos, but close to Arcadia and accessible from that region.) The purpose of these doors is an enigma. At Lykosoura the door opens onto a confined space, behind which are several extended rows of steps. At Bassai, the door faces a low mound of natural rock. The arrangement at Tegea is not clear, for the area to the north has not been excavated. The evidence, then, is slight, but it indicates a ritual purpose, a procession into the temple (hence the need for the ramp at Tegea and the steps at Lykosoura) watched by spectators standing along the side of the building (hence the steps at Lykosoura, and a possible function for the rock mound at Bassai). Further than this we cannot go, for we are straining the evidence already. Exactly what the ritual was must remain uncertain.

The impression one gets from these temples—particularly noticeable in the earliest of them, at Bassai—is that a strong local religious tradition has been accommodated to forms and architectural ideas introduced in emulation of other sanctuaries in other parts of Greece. The old, long, narrow archaic temple at Bassai, with its probable sequence of porch, cella and inner room has been clothed with the trappings of a conventional Doric peripteral structure, while retaining the elongated shape. The standard (and structurally pointless) false porch has been added at the south end, and the inner room reconciled with the simpler cella by the device of using the inner colonnades to define two distinct areas within the cella. It is a pity that we do not know more about the sanctuary here, in addition to the imposing temple. At Lykosoura the other arrangements of the sanctuary are fairly conventional, with portico and altars in front of the temple; but by Hellenistic times the conventional forms for a religious sanctuary were more universally accepted.

8   East Greek sanctuaries

The Greeks seem to have established themselves on the east coast of the Aegean during the late Bronze Age, probably as traders, possibly as the overlords of communities which were essentially non-Greek in origin (fig. 21). This Greek involvement may have been interrupted at the end of the thirteenth century, but even if this was so, the interruption was brief and was soon followed by the arrival of new Greek settlers, refugees from the troubled Greek mainland.[1] They arrived long before the development of the classical sanctuaries of the mainland; and the history of the sanctuaries in this area, though obviously related to that of the mainland, displays certain differences.

First, the east Greek communities had a mixed population, partly Greek, partly descended from the indigenous populations, Lydians, Carians and others. The latter obviously had their own attitudes and religious beliefs, and since the Greeks were particularly conscious of the local aspect of the gods, they naturally assimilated much of this local religion. Even if the gods have Greek names (or names that are the same as those of the Greek pantheon, which are not themselves necessarily Greek in origin), the form of worship and the powers which the gods exercise may rather be derived from the local tradition. Particularly significant in this respect seems to be the concept that the places of the gods were hallowed by tradition and ritual, rather than by monuments and buildings.

Secondly, though the east Greeks were subject to the same orientalizing influences which came to Greece with the redevelopment of trade contacts in the eighth century BC, they made their own particular selection of oriental elements for their own designs; in architecture, the most noticeable effect of this was the selection of the more decorative Syro-Phoenician volute capital, a form which was to evolve into the volute capitals of the north-eastern Aeolian area, and the more important Ionic capital.

Thirdly, the east Greeks were themselves subjected to different political influences. The sanctuaries were established by the late seventh century, in the period of independence, but they were then largely primitive in form, their architecture less developed than that of the most advanced communities. At the outset of the sixth century the communities on the mainland passed under the general control of the kings of Lydia. This was on the whole benevolent (though Miletus suffered and Smyrna was destroyed), despite the probability that the Lydians were of the same origin as the non-Greek element in many of the Greek cities. This resulted in the abnormal development of certain sanctuaries, that of Artemis of Ephesos benefiting particularly from Lydian munificence. Though the off-shore islands (such as Samos) did not pass under Lydian control, this development was not without consequence there. Then, when Lydian power and wealth appeared to be at its height, the Persians destroyed the kingdom and took control; more remote than the Lydians and less sympathetic, their rule was more concerned with the extraction of revenue. The

21 *Opposite*, map of the east Greek area

TROY

PERGAMON

MYTILINE

OLD SMYRNA

CHIOS

TEOS

EPHESOS

MAGNESIA

SAMOS
HERAION   PRIENE

MILETOS

DIDYMA

RHODES

0   20   40   60   80   100 Km

sanctuaries suffered, including those of the off-shore islands which Persia succeeded in subduing. These events certainly deflected the architectural development of the area from what might have been its more natural course.

Three east Greek sanctuaries are of particular importance in the early period: Artemis of Ephesos, Apollo of Didyma at Miletus, and Hera on the island of Samos. After the final overthrow of Persian rule, following the conquests of Alexander, the Greek cities were mostly free, though under the influence (political and economic) of the successor kings, and occasionally under their direct control. The sanctuaries at Ephesos and Didyma continued to be of first importance, Samos much less so. An account is also given here of the sanctuary of Artemis at Magnesia, essentially a development of this Hellenistic age.

Samos, the Heraion

The island of Samos was settled by Ionian Greeks during the period of migration at the end of the Bronze Age. In historical times it is a purely Greek island, without any significant traces of a pre-Greek population. The city of Samos was situated on the south coast in clear view of the mainland, where Samos possessed the adjacent territory, and opposite the city of Miletus, which became both a rival and enemy of Samos. The city was based on a promontory, which served as a citadel and guarded an excellent harbour. As Samos became more important, the city spread over the lower slopes of the hills behind; these were eventually included in the area enclosed by the city walls. The promontory would have afforded a suitable site for the principal temple but though there was undoubtedly a temple on it, the most important Samian sanctuary was situated some four or five miles to the west, in the opposite corner of a fertile coastal plain which began at Samos town.

This sanctuary of Hera was situated by a small stream, the Imbrasos, in low-lying ground, liable to flood and perennially marshy.[2] In view of this unusual situation (similar, however, to that of the great sanctuary of Artemis at Ephesos) and its distance from Samos town, one must suppose that the place was already sacred when the Ionians first arrived. The area of the sanctuary was by a late Bronze Age fortified settlement, and though this was destroyed and abandoned at the end of the Bronze Age, a lingering tradition must have remained. The earliest sanctuary seems to have involved sacrifice in front of a sacred tree, the *Lygos*, rather than any building, a clear indication of a nature cult assimilated by the Greeks to their cult of Hera. The tree remained an essential part of the sanctuary to the end, even though it came to be overshadowed by the architectural developments of temple, altar and ancillary buildings.

The first important development belongs to the eighth century BC; the excavators believe the date to be about 800 BC, though the possibility of a later date, still in the eighth century, should not be excluded. A long, narrow temple, 108 by 21 feet (32·8 by 6·4 metres), was built, of mud brick on stone footings, and with a single row of wooden posts down the centre to support the roof beams. There was no external colonnade, and the building represents the first stage in the development of temple architecture, when all that was technically possible in order to make the temple a more impressive building was to increase its length. This temple was eventually widened by means of a surrounding colonnade of wooden columns, five columns across the front, the odd number enabling a centre column to be lined up with the central columns in the cella. There was an altar in front of the temple, and a simple propylon to the north of this, where the road across the plain from the city entered the sanctuary. The Lygos tree formed the southern extremity of the sacred area.

In the seventh century there was considerable development. Thucydides had some knowledge of a division of the Greek world into two systems of alliance in about this period. The exact interpretation of this is difficult, but it is noticeable that he implies during this time close connections between Samos and Corinth.[3] Significantly, Samos rebuilt the Heraion as a stone temple (though still with wooden columns) with terracotta tiles at about the same time that Corinth was building the first stone temples to Apollo in the city and Poseidon at the Isthmus. This new temple, the second *hekatompedon*, was built on the same position as the first. The principal difference was the removal of the inner row of columns, though, unnecessarily, wall timbers were retained just inside the stone walls. The sanctuary was tidied up and improved. There was now a substantial altar, a more complex propylon, an enclosing wall for the Lygos tree, and, bordering the west side of the area between the temple and the tree, an extended stoa, 230 feet (69·9 metres) in length, with a double row of wooden posts, and two internal walls dividing its length into three sections. More minor monuments were constructed—small temples to other gods or treasuries—and groups of statues, often over life-size, by the side of the road. By the early sixth century the sanctuary was well endowed, with buildings, statues and other offerings.

The temple, however, was still essentially of eighth-century size. The decision was then taken to enlarge the temple to colossal dimensions. The chronology and the motivation for this are not certain. The ultimate inspiration was probably to be sought in the multi-columned temples of Egypt, though the new building was essentially an enlargement of the earlier Greek type, not a direct copy of the differently arranged Egyptian temples. Samos had established close relations with Egypt during this period; particularly in the reign of the Pharaoh Amasis, a usurper who relied greatly on Greek support, and whose reign seems officially to have begun in 570 BC. It was certainly about this time that the new temple was started; perhaps inspired by Egyptian models, and made possible by the flourishing condition of Samos at this time. It seems preferable to argue that this was the first of the larger temples, and that the comparable temple at Ephesos, financed in part at least by the Lydian King Croesus, who did not succeed to the Lydian throne until 560 BC, was second, inspired by the Samian temple, employing the same architect, and perhaps representing a propaganda exercise by Croesus, to demonstrate to the Greeks who were his subjects that he could benefit them as much as the connections of the free Greeks on the off-shore islands.

The temple was built on a low platform of two steps only. The position of the east front was determined by the site of the altar (which, although rebuilt, was not moved) and the greatly increased length of the new temple was achieved only by diverting the Imbrasos, and building in the reclaimed marshy land. The resulting platform measured approximately 174 by 314 feet (52·9 by 95·5 metres) or 171 by 311 feet (52·0 by 94·6 metres), presumably, on the top step, that is, over three times the size of the earlier temple. The colonnade was set back about ten feet from the edge of the top step. The temple was built of stone, walls and, now, columns; the tiles, of Corinthian

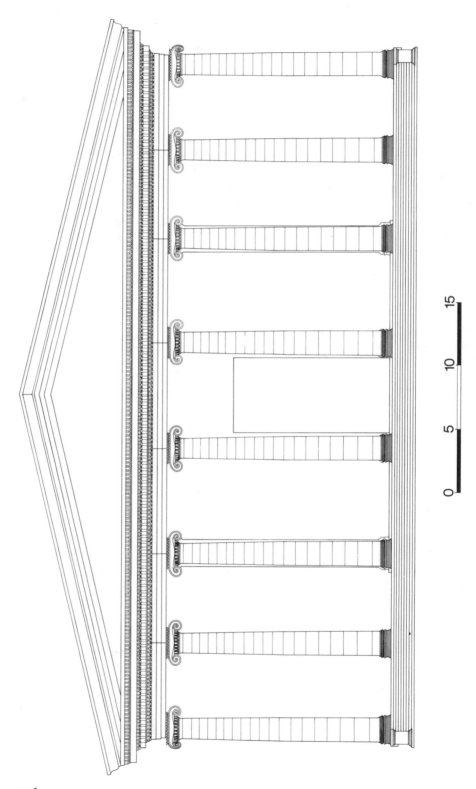

type, were of terracotta. The greatly enlarged dimensions were achieved by multiplying the rows of columns as much as by increasing the size of the cella building. There were now eight columns across the façade, with double rows to either side of the cella. The spacing between the façade columns was graduated, 17 feet (5·2 metres) axis to axis for the two outer spaces, 24 feet (7·3 metres) for the next space, 28 feet (8·5 metres) for the central space; this variation became an established feature of east Greek (Ionic) architecture. There was a deep porch, with two rows of columns; these also extended down the length of the cella.

The architects of the temple were Rhoikos and Theodoros. Theodoros wrote a treatise about it, which was known to the Roman architect Vitruvius.[4] It is difficult to distinguish the work of the two men, but Theodoros appears to have been concerned with the technical problems of building such a massive structure on marshy and, in part, reclaimed ground, and above all, the turning of the immense number of stone columns. Pliny suggests that it was Theodoros who invented a form of lathe which made this possible.[5] He also refers to the temple as 'The Labyrinth', indicating that the inspiration was probably the Egyptian temple by Lake Moeris, referred to by Herodotus under that name.[6]

Spectacular though this temple was, it had a short life, being destroyed by fire about 530 BC, presumably as the result of an accident (fig. 22). The rebuilding was initiated under the auspices of the tyrant of Samos, Polykrates, at a time when relations with Amasis of Egypt were made even closer by the threat to both now presented by the Persian empire. The new temple was to be even larger, the platform measuring 179 by 365 feet (54·4 by 111·0 metres), the extra length being achieved by three rows of columns at either end. The platform itself was higher, standing on ten steps, and was situated some distance to the west of Rhoikos' temple, which was razed to the ground. If completed, Polykrates' temple would have been the largest in Greece; but in 525 Egypt was conquered by Persia, and the Samians, isolated, soon had to come to terms with Persian power. Samos was ruined financially, and construction work was limited to the cella and porch, the internal colonnade, and the three rows of columns immediately in front of the porch. (It is possible that the cella, at this early stage, did not receive its inner colonnades and remained unroofed in consequence.) Peristyle columns were not added until Hellenistic times; work was still in progress in the Roman period, but the outer colonnade was never added.

The sanctuary was enhanced by the construction of temples to Hermes and Aphrodite, Apollo and Artemis, the latter being a substantial building. The other monuments, of Polykrates' time and during the preceding period, again include many statues, of which some in stone have survived.

Ephesos, the sanctuary of Artemis

The sanctuary of Artemis at Ephesos requires some comment, even though excavation has been limited to the temple—one of the original 'seven wonders of the world'—and the adjacent altar.[7] The site lies outside the city, or rather outside both the earlier

22 *Opposite*, the temple of Hera, Samos: reconstruction

city (situated on a nearby hill) and the more substantial Hellenistic and Roman city, a mile or so to the south-east. Since antiquity the water levels have changed; the estuary which made Ephesos an important harbour town has silted up, and the ground-water risen. The sanctuary is on low-lying ground, liable to flood, and the original excavation was carried out under great difficulty. The temple was buried to a considerable depth, and water had to be pumped continuously from the lower levels. The resulting hole in the ground is liable to fill with water, and even though it dries out in summer, the level revealed is only that of the latest, and highest, temple. (Recently, the Turkish authorities have re-erected one of the columns from this temple.) It is clear that the waterlogged nature of the site was causing trouble even in antiquity, for when this last temple was built (after the destruction of the sixth-century predecessor by a fire deliberately started by a maniac) the opportunity was taken to raise the platform on which it stood.

The low-lying, marshy site is obviously similar to that of Hera on Samos and presumably reflects the particular needs of a local cult, established before the Greek settlement. Whether the goddess was already called Artemis, or whether the Greeks applied to her a name with which they were already familiar, and which seemed appropriate to the particular aspect of the divinity worshipped there is quite uncertain. The cult-statue (of which there are copies and other representations, but not the original) is of a formal and unnaturalistic type, covered with protruberances which have been variously interpreted as female breasts or eggs; whatever the interpretation, the implication is of a goddess who promoted fertility.

The cult, then, is likely to have been old-established. Pausanias says that the temple of Artemis was older than the Greek migration, having been founded by the Amazons, the warrior women of Greek myth who helped the Trojans against their Greek enemies.[8] Traces of earlier temples were found under the first major building, the temple of the sixth century BC. These comprise a series of stone bases and foundations, the earliest being perhaps merely a sacred enclosure (though this is far from certain). One base, well built in ashlar masonry, contained a deposit of valuable objects. These were probably not a deliberate foundation deposit (buried in the same way that we conceal objects under a foundation stone) but a residue of gifts made to Artemis in her sanctuary, before the base was built. These stone structures and foundations hardly go back beyond 700 BC. The earliest of them cuts into the natural alluvial sand which underlies the whole sanctuary, but it may not have been the first religious building on the site. In this difficult place, the excavators could well have missed earlier, slighter structures.

For the later of these structures which underlie the sixth-century temple it is probable that a developed plan, of cella and at least a colonnaded porch, was already employed. Nothing of its superstructure remains. The replacement of this temple began a little before the middle of the sixth century. The earlier temple may have been destroyed or deliberately taken down; whatever the reason, the opportunity was seized to build a more splendid structure, rivalling Rhoikos' temple at the Samian Heraion, and perhaps reflecting the political differences between Ephesos, now flourishing as a much favoured part of the empire of the Lydian King Croesus, and the still-independent island of Samos. The connection between Ephesos and Lydia is emphasized by the fact that Croesus contributed to the construction of the new temple,

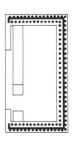
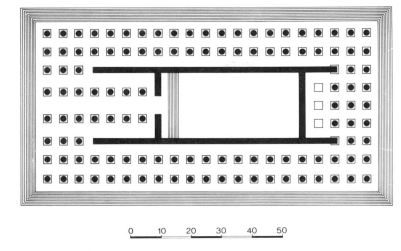

0   10   20   30   40   50

23 The altar (left) and temple of Artemis, Ephesos: sixth century

and his name appears as a dedicant on decorated column drums which survive from it, now in the British Museum. The connection with Samos is demonstrated by the fact that Theodoros, who had collaborated with Rhoikos on the Samian temple, is also one of the architects (with Chersiphron of Knossos in Crete and his son Metagenes) at Ephesos.

The temple these architects designed, like its immediate predecessors, faced west; this is not unusual for temples of Artemis, unlike those dedicated to other gods (fig. 23). It stood on a low platform of only two steps and measured on the top step 180½ by 377½ feet (55·1 by 115·14 metres), but this does not give the true size of the temple, for the columns were set well back from the edge. The similarities to the arrangements at Samos are obvious. Contrary to the usual Greek practice of making foundations only under colonnades and walls, this temple had a completely solid platform; presumably this is to be explained by the nature of the ground on which it stood. There were eight columns across the façade, and, probably, twenty-one along the side. The space between the façade columns increased towards the centre, the outer spacing measuring just over 20 feet (6·1 metres), the central spacing just over 28 feet (8·5 metres). At the rear were nine columns, the inner spacings there being reduced in consequence to just under 19 feet (5·8 metres). Several fragments of the columns were found by the excavators, and these show that the form of the Ionic column and capital had not yet been standardized. The columns were fluted, but the number of flutings varied—some had 40, others 44 or even 48. The capitals varied too. Some had rosettes instead of the usual volute pattern, and a palmette band round the top of the shaft. All were considerably narrower than classical capitals. These abnormal capitals are probably those from the façade, where the columns also had special bases, high drums carved with figure scenes in relief; it is these that bear Croesus' dedicatory inscriptions. Behind the outer colonnade came a second row of columns.

It has been suggested that, because of the distance between the two central columns of the façade, the entablature was of wood; but later authors refer to the difficulties

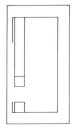

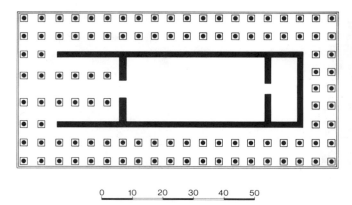

24 The altar (left) and temple of Artemis, Ephesos: fourth century (after the version of A. Bammer)

the architects experienced in lifting the central architrave block into place. Indeed, the achievement of this task was attributed to Artemis herself. As the architects are said by Vitruvius to have written a handbook describing their work, the difficulties were presumably real ones, and we must therefore suppose that the architrave, like the rest of the temple, was of marble.[9] It is not unlikely that the centre part of the pediment, which came over the central spacing, was left open in the form of a window. This would have relieved pressure on the central block, which otherwise might have cracked. Certainly the upper parts of the entablature were of stone. There would not have been a continuous frieze over the architrave, only the normal small dentils. Above the dentils came a cornice, and this was of a form not used after the sixth century BC. The outer edge of the cornice blocks was extended upwards to form a parapet, nearly three feet high, carved with figure scenes in relief. These were of marble, but similar cornices of terracotta, also of sixth-century date, are in the Birmingham City Museum. In later Ionic architecture the cornices are much simpler and the continuous frieze is brought down either to replace the dentils altogether, or, in the Hellenistic age, to form an additional ornament between the dentils and the architrave.

The plan of the cella is not absolutely certain. Plans published in the handbooks are often more assured than the facts warrant.[10] The side walls were certainly aligned with the third column of the façade. They ran forward to form a deep porch, but probably ended without the antae that were normal in Doric architecture, and were eventually, perhaps under Doric influence, used in Ionic buildings. Between the side walls of the porch were four pairs of columns. The effect, on entering the temple, must have been that of a veritable forest of columns, and the influence of Egyptian architecture, which also massed columns in this way, is apparent. It is generally assumed that there was a false porch at the rear. This is not a usual Ionic feature, and as it is not found in the sixth-century temples of Hera on Samos and of Apollo at Didyma its presence at Ephesos may also be doubted. The most recent study of the temple suggests instead an inner room or *adyton* at the back of the cella.[11] This study has also made revolutionary suggestions concerning the roof of the temple, but these are best discussed after the account of the later building. The main room contained the cult-statue, which seems to have stood on a base directly over, but larger than, those of the earlier temples.

Croesus was defeated by Cyrus of Persia in 546 BC, having been tempted to offer battle, according to the legend, by a misleading prophecy from the oracle at Delphi. His kingdom then became a province of the Persian empire. Therefore the temple must have been begun before the middle of the sixth century, and the primitive form of its Ionic order supports this date. It has been suggested that the details of the cornice parapet relief indicate that work continued into the fifth century BC. This is possible, for with Croesus' wealth cut off, the Greek cities were in a less favourable position under the Persians, and Miletus, an old enemy of the Lydians who had quickly gone over to the Persian side, seems to have supplanted the Lydian favourite Ephesos as the most prosperous among them. However, the Persians respected the religious practices and shrines of their subjects, destroying them only as an act of vengeance after rebellion or a particularly stubborn resistance to their conquests, and work on the temple may well have continued after Ephesos became subject to Persia.

Altogether the temple stood for close on two hundred years, far longer than its rivals, the temple of Hera on Samos built by Rhoikos, burnt down after a mere forty years or so, and the temple of Apollo at Didyma in the territory of Miletus, destroyed by the Persians after their erstwhile favourite had rebelled against them. The temple of Artemis was fired by a maniac called Herostratos in 356 BC, and the Greeks, who loved coincidences of this sort, afterwards discovered that this happened on the day that Alexander the Great was born.

The replacement of the ruined temple seems to have begun almost immediately, and naturally the new building was placed directly on the site of the old, utilizing but enlarging slightly the old platform (fig. 24). The new platform was much higher than the old, having ten steps in place of the original two, thus raising the building higher above its marshy surroundings, but also giving it a base more in accordance with the developed proportions of Ionic temples of the fourth century BC. It is possible that the interior of the cella was left at the old level thus requiring a flight of steps leading down to its floor from the porch, for a Roman foundation was later laid at that level. The plan of the new temple seems to have followed that of the old, and it was almost exactly the same length. At its west end, however, it was extended a little, giving space for three rows of columns in front of the porch where previously there had only been two. The lower level of the cella floor raises a further possibility caused by the fact that any columns standing on it would have needed to be 9 feet 2 inches (2·79 metres) higher (the difference between the old and new platform levels) to reach the same ceiling level as the exterior and porch columns. From this it has been argued that the cella was unroofed, certainly in the later temple and—from the way the later copies the older arrangement in essentials—probably in the earlier temple.[12] This would make the temple, appropriately in view of its great fame, the essential precedent for the similar roofless cella, approached (nominally, at least) by a flight of steps leading down from the porch, found in the temple of Apollo at Didyma. Attractive though these theories are, given our inadequate knowledge of the temple and its very poor state of preservation, they cannot be accepted as proven or, indeed, provable.

Of the structures outside the temple the only important remains belong to the altar. This consists of a large rectangular foundation, almost as wide as the temple platform, placed on an axial alignment directly opposite the west end of the temple, and enclosing a ramp. Again, its exact restoration is a matter of conjecture, but from its shape it could well be a colonnaded altar, similar in principle to that which was erected, on a more elaborate scale, to Zeus at Pergamon. The theory that the arrangement was in some way connected with a revelation of the cult-statue in the central window of the pediment is speculative.[13]

The temple is tantalizing for the archaeologist who appreciates its importance and the quality of the fragments (particularly the carved column drums of both the old and new temple). Nothing now visible on the site would lead one to realize that it was once one of the seven wonders of the world. Its destruction results from its abandonment outside the late antique and medieval fortress towns that succeeded the classical city. To be pillaged as a quarry in the period of the early Christian empire was, perhaps, a fair requital for the treatment St Paul received from the priests and devotees of Diana (the Roman counterpart of Artemis) of the Ephesians.

Didyma, the sanctuary of Apollo

The sanctuary of Apollo at Didyma lay some ten miles south of Miletus, to which city it belonged, at the south-western corner of the Milesian promontory.[14] It is now surrounded by a Turkish village, called Didim (an artificial name derived deliberately from the ancient; before 1922 the village was Greek, and was called Ieronda, that is, the sacred place). The former Greek Orthodox church, now converted into a mosque, lies by the ancient sanctuary, and it seems clear that there was here a real continuity of religious usage, from pre-Greek to post-Greek times. We do not know how the Greek population of Miletus was distributed geographically, but in an outlying part like Didyma a strong and continuing Carian element is likely. The fact that the principal sanctuary of the Milesians is not situated in the city indicates that it had a pre-Greek origin. The temple itself is one of the major monuments of antiquity, but little of its sanctuary is now visible. It is approached now, as then, by a road running south from Miletus itself, across the undulating Milesian peninsula. The road runs down to a beach, the ancient landing place for pilgrims travelling by sea. From here a ceremonial 'sacred way' led up to the temple, which towered on the top of a low hill; the columns that survive intact can still be seen from a considerable distance, and urge on the traveller with the promise of antiquities on an extraordinary scale. He will not be disappointed.

From the landing place to the temple the sacred way was lined with large, uncouth statues of seated figures. A century ago many of them were still to be seen. Between sixty and seventy were counted in 1821, but now they have all disappeared, though ten survive at the British Museum and others elsewhere. These belonged to the archaic age of Greek art, and were survivors from the earlier temples. Their inspiration was, presumably, the Egyptian practice of placing carved figures by their processional ways.

The immediate predecessor of the surviving temple was built in the sixth century BC. It seems to have been comparable in scale, and probably in plan and general arrangement.[15] If so, it is an important antecedent for the peculiarities of the later temple, which might otherwise be attributed to the fact that it was left unfinished.

This archaic predecessor was deliberately destroyed by the Persians at the beginning of the fifth century. The cult-statue was taken by Darius, the Persian king, to his palace at Ecbatana, where it remained for almost two hundred years until it was restored to the Milesians following the conquest of the Persian empire by Alexander the Great, though it was one of the successors of Alexander, Seleucus, who was responsible for its restoration, wishing to gain the support of Miletus.

Nevertheless, it is likely that reconstruction of the temple had commenced before the restoration of the old cult-statue. It is unthinkable that the sanctuary had ceased to function for some two hundred years, and it is likely that rebuilding began as soon as Miletus' economy revived, presumably when the region was freed from Persian control by Alexander himself. Presumably the progress of reconstruction prompted Seleucus to return the old statue.

Externally the new structure appears to be a colossal, though unfinished, Ionic temple of more or less normal type (fig. 25). It has a high base with seven steps, each too high to be of practical use so the number is doubled in front for the entire width of the cella building (plate 45). On this base stood a façade of ten Ionic columns; they had particularly elaborate bases, with two examples of each. Down the sides were 21 columns, with the normal Asiatic type of base which had evolved in the sixth century. Unlike the sixth-century columns, however, these stood on square plinths. The columns were fluted, and had a height of over 64 feet (19·7 metres). There was an inner row of columns, all with Asiatic bases, along the sides and across the front and back.

From the outside the cella building which these colonnades surrounded was of normal type and of traditional Ionic form. At the front there was the usual deep Ionic porch, containing within the side walls three rows of four columns. There was no false porch at the rear. The ends of the porch walls, it is true, and the corners at the back had antae, which are not found in older Ionic architecture, but they had already been used in the temples of Zeus at Labraunda and of Athena at Priene. The wall dividing the porch from the interior was again apparently normal in design, with a large central doorway, elaborately framed, which must once have contained the usual two-leaf door found in all Greek temples; but here the resemblance to ordinary temple architecture ends. The threshold of the central door rises nearly five feet above the floor level of the porch in a single step. No human being could have entered the temple by that way. Instead, there are two minor and insignificant doors to either side at floor level. These do not lead directly into the cella, as they would in a normal temple, but into narrow vaulted, and sloping passages, which descend to the natural ground level. From this level the walls of the cella rise up, still impressive though they only survive for part of their original height (plate 46). In the position where the cult-statue would normally stand there was a small temple building, a shrine within a shrine, and it was in this that the cult-statue was placed.

The inner temple was also an Ionic structure, with a three-stepped base and four Ionic columns across the façade which reflected the type of the columns outside, having Asiatic bases on square plinths. Its entablature was ornate. The simple moulding that separates the architrave from the dentils was elaborated into a profiled frieze, carved with a palmette pattern. The architectural forms of this inner temple indicate that it was built about 300 BC and it has been suggested that it was to house the cult-

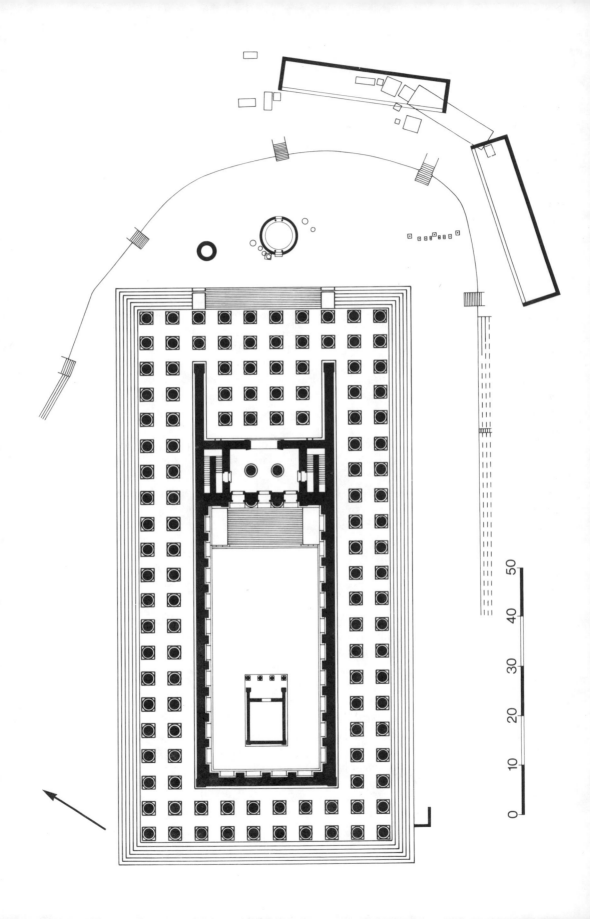

statue after its return from Ecbatana but before the main temple was completed. It now seems that such an inner shrine was already a feature in the earlier temple, and that it was an essential part of the original design.

Also an essential and abnormal part of the design is the interior arrangement at the eastern end of the cella. To either side are the openings from the entrance passages. Between them a flight of 24 steps, 50 feet wide (15.2 metres), rises to the floor level formed by the elevated threshold of the main door. Between the top of the steps and the door is a large room, with two internal columns to support its ceiling. The function of this room is not certain, but, unless the principal purpose of the wide staircase is mere decoration, one must assume that large numbers of people were expected to have access to it. To either side of this room are small doorways leading to stone staircases contained between the side walls of the room and the outer wall of the cella. These are narrow, and could only cope with a single file of people using them. They continue as high as the walls are preserved, and must once have reached even higher, but what they led to, and why, must remain completely obscure.

The inner sides of the cella walls are plain for a height of $17\frac{1}{2}$ feet (5.35 metres), that is, from the natural ground level to that of the floor in the room behind the main door. There is no indication whatever that it was intended to put a floor at this level over the entire cella, and such a floor is quite improbable. Above this level the walls were decorated with a series of pilasters, the capitals of which had flat front surfaces between volutes, a design that can be traced back to the sixth century BC. Between these capitals the wall surface was carved, the decoration consisting of foliage and griffins, mythical beasts again of archaic and eastern ancestry. The design returned at the east end for a space of one bay at either side, up to the line of the stair. Here the wall was interrupted by three doorways that led into the enclosed room. The two sections of wall between these doors were decorated not with pilasters, but with engaged Corinthian half-columns.

The temple obviously was never finished. Around the base of the cella wall, on the outside, it was intended that a moulded decoration should be carved, as is normal in Ionic architecture. The rough shape of it was cut on the blocks before they were put in position, but only at the end of the walls was the decoration completed. The rest was left blank, and so it remains to the present day. It is also assumed, from the poor work and design of some of the details, that construction was extended over a very long period indeed, and that it was probably continued even when Miletus lost its independence and became part of the Roman empire.

The temple was never roofed. If it had been, the differences between it and the normal Greek temple would not have been so considerable. Eccentricities of plan could well be explained by the oracular function the building is supposed to have performed. A temple without a roof is a different matter. In the nineteenth century, following hints given by Vitruvius, it used to be thought that there was a distinct category of temple that had no roof over the cella. Candidates for this category included the temple of Apollo at Bassai, and even the Parthenon itself. This was considered necessary in order that enough light should be admitted to a room totally devoid of windows to reveal the works of art contained within, the frieze at Bassai,

25 *Opposite*, the temple of Apollo, Didyma

the statue of Athena in the Parthenon. It was not realized that a gloomy, dark interior was more in keeping with the proper religious atmosphere, or that with the dazzling brilliance of Greek sunshine, sufficient light would be reflected through the great doors to illuminate the interior of the cella.

It is now usually considered that temples without roofs were simply uncompleted. The temple of Apollo at Didyma, superficially, is one such building. On the other hand, the internal arrangements of the cella do suggest that a roof was never intended. If it had been roofed, it would have been very dark and gloomy indeed, for in contrast to normal temples, as we have seen, the great east door does not open into the cella, but only into the anteroom. The amount of light which could pass through this room and the three smaller doors at the top of the inner staircase was small. The fraction of this light which could have entered the inner shrine must have been infinitesimal. Since it would seem that the interior of the cella was not lit by windows set high in the wall, we must assume that it was intended from the first that it should remain open to the sky. The similar plan of the archaic temple suggests that this was also true of the older building, and that this arrangement was a deliberate and essential feature at Didyma, not merely the result of the accident that the later building had to remain unfinished. A similar inner shrine exists in the (roofed) temple of Hemithea at Kastabos, in southern Caria.[16]

Thus Didyma was from the start an anomalous building. The intention was to create the external appearance of a colossal, but otherwise normal, Ionic temple, but to conceal within this a temple of a radically abnormal type. We are told by the Greek geographer Strabo, writing in the first century BC, that the temple contained a grove of laurel bushes.[17] Not far distant from Miletus, in that part of Caria which was not under Greek control, the chief Carian sanctuary at Labraunda consisted, at least in the fifth century BC, of a grove of trees; it was only in the fourth century that the dynasty of Hecatomnos built a temple of Greek type.[18] It seems likely that when the first colossal temple of Apollo was constructed at Didyma, imitating those of the other Ionian cities but in a region where part at least of the population was probably of Carian ancestry, it was found impossible to obliterate a sacred grove, the religious significance of which long antedated the development of the classical temple. So the sacred grove had to remain. The temple had to be built round the grove, and as the laurels needed light and water, no roof was possible. It was not until after the time of Strabo, when the significance of the grove had at last been lost, that it was removed and the interior of the cella paved.

On the other hand it might be doubted whether even a roofless cella, when the walls had reached their full height, would have admitted enough light to enable the laurels to flourish. Possibly Strabo meant that the laurels were in the sanctuary, rather than the inner construction of the temple. It is unfortunate that a detailed investigation of the sanctuary and the setting of the temple has not been possible. Only one monument of any importance has been revealed, a circular foundation in front of the east end of the temple. This is generally assumed, from its position rather than any positive evidence, to have been the altar, but, if so, its shape is anomalous.

Magnesia, the sanctuary of Artemis

The ancient city of Magnesia ad Maendrum now lies some miles inland, north-east of the modern Turkish town of Söke. In antiquity the estuary of the Maeander river, which is now silted up, extended to the territory of Magnesia, so that the ancient Greek settlement there, like all those in this part of the world, had lands by the sea. The settlement formed part of the Ionian migration to the east in the dark ages, but, like its neighbour Priene, it seems not to have coalesced into a recognizable urban community until about the fourth century BC. The city then created was laid out like Miletus and Priene, with a regular alignment of streets on a grid plan. This was partly excavated at the end of the last century, and the central area of the city cleared, revealing the agora and the adjacent and principal religious sanctuary dedicated to Artemis Leukophryene, Artemis of the White Elbow.[19] This sanctuary and its temple were famous in antiquity. It is mentioned admiringly by the geographer Strabo and referred to by Vitruvius in his handbook of architecture.[20] Strabo considered it one of the most beautiful temples, and though modern opinion would not echo this, it was clearly both an important and an imposing building (fig. 26).

Moreover, it was the work of a very famous architect, Hermogenes of Priene. Hermogenes is a controversial figure in the history of Greek architecture. He lived during the first part of the second century BC (the temple of Artemis dates, probably, to about the middle of the century) and thus belongs to a period when the Greek world was in decline. Asia Minor, where he lived and worked, was at that time virtually divided between the kings of Pergamum (Attalos II) and the Greek city of Rhodes, both of whom had served the Romans faithfully in their wars against Philip V of Macedon and Antiochos III. Their extended political power and wealth was a reward granted them by the goodwill of the Roman Senate. Hermogenes not only built temples but wrote books about them; his attitudes to architecture were known and approved by his successors, and they obviously had some effect on his buildings. He is most famous for his rejection of the Doric order, as being too faulty to be suitable for temples, and he was probably responsible for a very real revival of interest in the Ionic order, of which Artemis Leukophryene affords an excellent example; significantly, the Doric order is reduced to the subordinate role of serving for the columns of the stoas which surround and enclose the temple courtyard.[21]

Magnesia is on a low-lying, marshy site, though there are hills immediately behind it; not the obvious or natural place for a Greek city. The sanctuary temple and the surrounding courtyard is noticeably on a different alignment to the grid plan of the town, exemplified by the adjacent agora. It is very strange that the sanctuary breaks the regularity of the grid plan; at neighbouring Priene the sanctuary of Athena is fully aligned with the street grid. It is even more curious because there was obviously a close relationship between the sanctuary and the agora; the principal approach to the sanctuary is from the agora. It is true that the discrepancy is probably more noticeable on paper than it would have been when the two courtyards, agora and sanctuary were complete, and when it would have been difficult to see from one to the other, and so relate them visually. The lack of alignment would have been slightly noticed in the sanctuary, where exceptionally the west boundary is not at right angles to the others.

137

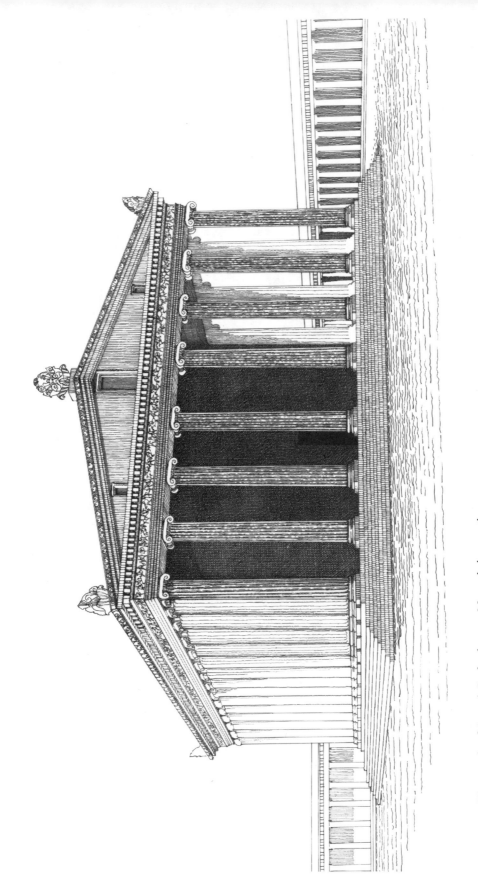

26 The temple of Artemis Leukophryene, Magnesia (perspective reconstruction)

There are two possible explanations of this, which may in fact be complementary to each other. The alignment of the temple and altar was probably determined by cult and ritual requirements, while the town planner wanted his streets to be aligned with the cardinal points of the compass. The temple needed to be aligned with, perhaps, the setting sun (since it faces west) or with some aspect of the moon, whose deity Artemis was. The other factor is the probability that the sanctuary existed before the town was created, though it seems strange that the town street grid did not follow the alignment of the temple. That the sanctuary was an old one is very likely. It is in low-lying marshy ground, of the type of position favoured by the greater temple of Artemis at Ephesos, and it may well be that it was the existence of the sanctuary that led to this site being chosen for the new city of Magnesia.

The plan of the sanctuary is extremely simple. The sides are exactly parallel to each other, the east end being at right angles to them. All have Doric colonnades in front of them, except the west end, which follows the differing alignment of the agora, and has no colonnade. These colonnades thus create an unbroken setting round the temple, with none of the variety or interruptions normal around the edge of a Greek sanctuary. The concept of the colonnaded court, of space enclosed by building, which was present in Greek architecture with the developed houses and other courtyard buildings from at least the sixth century BC, is here asserting itself in the context of religious architecture, where the previous idea, that of the free-standing building surrounded by space, had usually prevailed. There is, of course, also a temple of traditional appearance, with its peristyle of Ionic columns set on top of the normal stepped base, designed to be viewed from all directions as much as was the Parthenon or any other classical building. Its columns are substantially taller than those of the surrounding colonnade, and the temple would obviously have been the most spectacular and noticeable building in the sanctuary. Yet the colonnades of the courtyard at the side and the back, positioned at a distance of 92 and 112 feet (28 and 34 metres) from the bottom step of the temple, distinctly hem it in and give little free space for the major structure except from the front. Here there is a more extensive space, needed for ritual purposes and containing a substantial, colonnaded altar, set on the central axial alignment. The entrance to the sanctuary, the propylon-style structure incorporated into the surrounding portico of the agora, is also placed on this same alignment.

The sense of order and arrangement in this sanctuary is obviously great. When it was complete, one suspects that the effect may have been a little stifling—even overpowering, with the distinctly restricted space around the altar hemmed in by the colonnades to the side and dominated by the towering façade of the temple. It is noticeable that the temple façade would have created much more impact than the rest of the temple, and although, clearly, this sanctuary is still some way from the Roman concept, where the temple simply is a façade set at the very back of a court and with the steps restricted to the façade, it is closer to this than to the original Greek idea. Whether Hermogenes was, consciously or unconsciously, receptive of Roman influence may be seriously doubted. It is more likely that the influence came from the planned sanctuaries of the Hellenistic cities in Syria or Egypt, and from a tendency, noticeable in the agora at Magnesia in contrast to the earlier east Greek agoras at Priene and Miletus, to enclose the courtyard, to divert streets to pass outside rather than through, and to create distinct entrances with formal doorways. Nevertheless, it shows equally a tendency towards something similar to the Roman idea of the temple court—it is more than possible that developed Roman temple planning owed much to these Hermogenean ideas—which enabled the Greek world to accept the Roman temple, with its podium, and steps restricted to one end.

Notes

ABBREVIATIONS

AA   *Archäologischer Anzeiger*
Ath. Mitt.   *Mitteilungen des deutschen archäologischen Instituts; athenische Abteilung*
BCH   *Bulletin de Correspondence Hellénique*
BSA   *Annual of the British School of Athens*
Hesperia   *Hesperia*: Journal of the American School of Classical Studies at Athens
IG   *Inscriptiones Graecae*
JDI   *Jahrbuch des deutschen archäologischen Instituts*
Jahreshefte   *Jahreshefte des Österreichischen archäologischen Instituts*
JHS   *Journal of Hellenic Studies*

I INTRODUCTION—THE BRONZE AGE

1   V. R. d'A. Desborough, *The Greek Dark Ages* (London, 1972), and A. M. Snodgrass, *The Dark Age of Greece* (Edinburgh, 1972), are the latest full discussions of this period.

2   For the language, M. Ventris and J. Chadwick, *Documents in Mycenaean Greek* (Cambridge, 1956); for the palace communities (and late Bronze Age civilization in general), E. Vermeule, *Greece in the Bronze Age* (Chicago, 1964); A. J. B. Wace and F. H. Stubbings, *A Companion to Homer* (London, 1962).

3   Herodotus II 50: the names of nearly all the gods came to Greece from Egypt.

4   For these developments, see J. Boardman, *The Greeks Overseas*, 2nd ed. (Harmondsworth, 1973), chapters 3 and 4.

5   E. Vermeule, Chapter IX.

6   Preliminary reports in *Archaeological Reports* 1968/9 p. 11 f; 1969/70 p. 12 f.

7   J. Caskey, *Hesperia*, 1964 p. 326 f.

8   E. Vermeule, p. 283

9   B. Bergquist, *Herakles on Thasos* (Uppsala, 1973), esp. p. 23 f.

10 The idea that there is continuity in religion from the Bronze Age into the first millennium is argued fully and forcibly by M. P. Nilsson, in his *The Minoan and Mycenaean religions* (esp. part II pp. 447–633 in the second edition, Lund, 1950) and in his *The Mycenaean Origin of Greek Mythology* (Berkeley, 1932). Recent opinion (e.g. A. Snodgrass, pp. 394–399) is more sceptical. This scepticism is based primarily on the lack of archaeological evidence for continuity, and evidence that certain practices were discontinued, such as the deposition of terracotta goddess figurines. The argument from Delos that there was continuity (Gallet de Santerre, *Délos primitive et archaique*—Paris, 1958) is suspect, because the religious nature of the evidence is doubtful. Nevertheless, this scepticism seems overdone, since it is concerned only with material evidence; beliefs and even cults could well survive without leaving durable remains, particularly if, in a time of scarcity of manufactured goods, the offerings to the gods were of an essentially perishable nature, in sanctuaries devoid of permanent structures.

2 THE SANCTUARIES OF THE CLASSICAL AGE

1 e.g. Stuart and Revett, *The Antiquities of Athens* (4 vols., London, 1762–   ), and the Dilettanti Society's *The Antiquities of Ionia* (5 vols, London, 1797–   ).
2 Beginning with Winkelmann, whose *Gedanken über die Nachahmung des Griechischen Werke* was published in 1755.
3 J. Mordaunt Cook, *The Greek Revival* (London, 1970).
4 'Cow and panoply', B. D. Meritt and H. T. Wade-Gery, *JHS* 1962 p. 69.
5 Plutarch, *Alcibiades* 34; Plato, *Euthyphro* 6c.
6 *IG* i² 24.
7 B. Bergquist, *The Archaic Greek Temenos* (Lund, 1967), pp. 61 and 104 f.
8 B. Bergquist, *Herakles on Thasos*.
9 Except for plain wares used locally.
10 Examples: *IG* i² 268 (Meiggs and Lewis, *Selection of Greek Historical Inscriptions* no. 76)—Athens. *IG* 11 287—Delos.
11 Effectively, by Theodosius the Great in AD 392.
12 For example, the sixth-century temple of Apollo at Corinth.

3 THE BUILDINGS

1 H. G. G. Payne, *Perachora* I (Oxford, 1940), p. 34 f.
2 See, for example, the section of the temple of Hephaistos (the Theseum), A. T. Hodge, *The Woodwork of Greek Roofs* (Cambridge, 1960), fig. 4.
3 R. M. Dawkins, *Artemis Orthia* (London, 1929), p. 11.
4 Hermione (Porto Cheli): *Archaeological Reports* 1971/2, p. 9. Boeotia: the temple at Aulis: *Archaeological Reports* 1960/1, p. 15; the temple on Mount Mavrovouni, J. M. Fossey and R. A. Tomlinson, *BSA* 1970, p. 245. Sicily: plans in W. B. Dinsmoor, *The Architecture of Ancient Greece* (London, 1950), fig. 28.
5 Compare the temple models from Perachora (above, note 1) with any classical temple.
6 P. Zancani Montuoro and V. Zanotti-Bianco, *Heraion alle Foce del Sele* (Rome, 1954).
7 Particularly the 'Treasury of Atreus' at Mycenae. Some tholoi are of much less careful masonry.
8 *BSA* 1958/59, p. 97.
9 e.g. Dinsmoor, plate XVII (Thermon).
10 V. Karageorghis, *BCH* 1970, p. 377 f.
11 In stone form, over the Lion Gate at Mycenae and flanking the doorway to the treasury at Atreus.
12 R. D. Barnett, *The Nimrud Ivories in the British Museum* (London, 1951), plate IV.
13 The latest discussion: R. M. Cook, 'The Archetypal Doric Temple', *BSA* 1970, p. 17.
14 Dinsmoor, plate XIX.
15 'Triglyphs' on ivories: R. D. Barnett, plates XXXIII and XXXIV.
16 F. C. Penrose, *An Investigation of the Principles of Athenian Architecture*, 2nd ed. (London, 1888).
17 It is mentioned in Thucydides' account of the Kylonian conspiracy, which took place towards the end of the seventh century BC (i 126.10). Herodotus (V 71) speaks of the 'statue' of Athena.
18 G. Roux, *L'Architecture de l'Argolide* (Paris, 1961), p. 62 f.
19 H. Winnefeld, *Altertümer von Pergamon* III 2; E. Schmidt, *The Great Altar of Pergamon* (London, 1965).

20 H. Plommer and F. Salviat, 'The Altar of Hera Akraia at Perachora', *BSA* 1966, p. 207 f.
21 Dinsmoor, p. 287; C. G. Yavis, *Greek Altars* (St Louis, Miss., 1949), p. 189.
22 Labraunda: *Swedish Excavations and Researches*, Vol 1 part 1, 'The Propylaea' (K. Jeppesen).
23 Strabo 14 i 40.
24 Pausanias 6. 19. 1 (Olympia).
25 R. A. Tomlinson in *Ancient Macedonia* (ed. B. Laourdas and Ch. Makaronas) (Thessaloniki 1970), p. 308 f.
26 R. A. Tomlinson, *JHS* 1969, p. 106 f.; B. Bergquist, *Herakles on Thasos*.
27 Athenaeus IV 138 f.
28 B. Dunkley, 'Greek Fountain Buildings before 300 B.C.', *BSA* 1936.
29 R. A. Tomlinson, *BSA* 1969, p. 195 f., and in H. W. Catling, 'Archaeology in Greece', *Archaeological Reports* 1972/3, p. 8.

4 THE FINANCING OF SANCTUARIES

1 C. M. Kraay and M. Hirmer, *Greek Coins* (London, 1966), Introduction.
2 e.g. penalties involved in the reassessment of tribute by Athens, *IG* i² 63 (Meiggs Lewis no. 69).
3 B. Bergquist, *Herakles on Thasos*, p. 70 f.
4 Meiggs Lewis no. 59.
5 Plutarch, *Pericles* 12.
6 Aristotle, *Politics* 1291ᵃ 33–4; J. K. Davies, *Athenian Propertied Families*, Introduction, p. xx f.
7 SIG 239B, M. N. Tod, *Greek Historical Inscriptions* II no. 140.
8 The Delian accounts are on *IG* ii² 1635 Tod, no. 125.
9 Harpokration (see under Propylaia): Heliodoros says this cost 2012 talents.
10 A. Burford, *The Greek Temple Builders at Epidauros* (Liverpool, 1969).
11 R. S. Stanier, 'The cost of the Parthenon', *JHS* 1953, p. 68 f.
12 e.g. *IG* 11 287, from Delos.

5 MAJOR SANCTUARIES

1 Pausanias 5. 10. 2.
2 The intervention of King Pheidon of Argos: Pausanias 6. 22. 2.
3 Pausanias 10. 5. 3.
4 Herodotus I 50–51.
5 An up-to-date account of the sanctuary is A. Mallwitz, *Olympia und seine Bauten* (Munich, 1972).
6 Unless otherwise stated, the measurements of the outer dimensions of temples will be those taken at the stylobate.
7 Pausanias 5. 10. 2. Nothing else is known about him.
8 Pausanias 5. 10. 4. The inscription: Curtius and Adler, *Olympia* vol. 5, p. 253.
9 Stephen Miller, 'The Prytaneion at Olympia', *Ath. Mitt.* 1971, p. 79 f.
10 Delphi has been excavated since the late nineteenth century by the École Française d'Athènes; the results are published in *Fouilles de Delphes*.
11 H. W. Parke and D. Wormell, *The Delphic Oracle* (Oxford, 1956).
12 Herodotus V 62.
13 Pausanias 10. 11. 4. says Marathon.

14 R. Flacelière, *Les Aitoliens à Delphes* (Paris, 1937).

15 Cedrenus, p. 304a.

16 Gallet de Santerre, *Délos primitive et archaique*. The excavations at Delos (again the work of the École Française) are recorded in *Exploration archéologique de Délos*.

17 In the poems of Solon, quoted in Aristotle, *Constitution of Athens* 4. 2.

18 Dinsmoor, p. 184.

19 The battles of Kos and Andros.

6 OTHER IMPORTANT SANCTUARIES

1 e.g. E. Vermeule, plate XXIIIA.

2 O. Broneer, 'A Mycenaean Fountain on the Athenian Acropolis', *Hesperia* VIII p. 317 f.

3 For discussion of Athens in the Dark Age, see V. R. d'A. Desborough, *The Greek Dark Ages*.

4 Herodotus VIII 55.

5 See chapter 3, note 17.

6 H. Plommer, 'The Archaic Acropolis: some problems', *JHS* 1960, p. 127 f.

7 *IG* i² 372.

8 The archonship of Hippokleides: Eusebius (oL.58.3). The festival traditionally founded by Erichthonios (Harpokration, see under 'Panathenaia') or more usually Theseus (Plutarch, *Theseus* 24, Pausanias VIII 2.1.).

9 Herodotus VII 141.

10 Lycurgus, *Leocr.* 80 f.; Diodorus XI 29.2 f.

11 The 'Peace of Kallias'. For a full discussion (in favour of the idea that there was a formal peace), R. Meiggs, *The Athenian Empire* (Oxford, 1972), p. 487 f.

12 *IG* i² 24; Meiggs-Lewis, no. 44.

13 G. P. Stevens, 'The Periclean Entrance Court of the Acropolis', *Hesperia* 1936, p. 446 f.

14 J. Bundgaard, *Mnesicles* (Copenhagen, 1957), p. 30 f.; H. Plommer, *JHS* 1960, p. 148.

15 Pausanias 1. 22. 6.

16 J. Travlos, *Pictorial Dictionary of Ancient Athens* (London, 1971), p. 482 f.

17 Dinsmoor, p. 203.

18 Hence the generic term Mycenaean, often used for the late Bronze Age in Greece.

19 Pausanias 2. 19. 3.

20 C. Waldstein, *The Argive Heraeum* (Boston and New York, 1902), P. Amandry, *Hesperia* 1952, p. 222 f. The sanctuary is being restudied by the American School at Athens.

21 Kleomenes I: see Herodotus VI 81.

22 Amandry, *Hesperia* 1952, p. 222 f.

23 The first volume of the excavation report has been published, O. Broneer, *Isthmia* Vol 1, The Temple of Poseidon (Princeton, 1971).

24 See chapter 3 above, and note 4.

25 For a full study of its development, see A. Burford, *The Greek Temple Builders at Epidauros*.

26 Athens: J. Travlos, p. 127 f. (with full references). Corinth: C. Roebuck, *Corinth* XIV, the Asklepieion and Lerna.

27 Burford, p. 41 f.

28 R. A. Tomlinson, 'Two buildings in Sanctuaries of Asklepios', *JHS* 1969, p. 106 f.

29 G. Roux, p. 113.

30 Burford, p. 54.

31 Detailed discussion in F. Robert, *Thymélè* (Paris, 1939).

32 R. A. Tomlinson, *JHS* 1969, p. 106 f.

33 G. Roux, 277; Miss Burford (p. 69) prefers an earlier date.

34 A. von Gerkan and W. Müller-Wiener, *Das Theater von Epidauros* (Stuttgart, 1961). Miss Burford (p. 75) prefers the more usual dating of *c.* 360 BC.

7 LESSER SANCTUARIES

1 G. Welter, *Aigina* (Berlin, 1938).
2 G. Welter, *AA* 1938, col. 8 f.
3 The original excavations are published in A. Furtwängler, *Aegina: Das Heiligtum der Aphaia* (Munich, 1906).
4 Recent excavations confirm a date about 570: *BCH* 1970, p. 934; 1971 p. 842.
5 *Archaeological Reports* 1971/2 p. 9.
6 B. Bergquist, *The Archaic Greek Temenos*, p. 15 f.
7 In the Hellenistic age they were briefly restored to Nemea by Aratos of Sikyon in 235 BC (cf. Plutarch, *Aratos* 28.3).
8 The temple at Nemea is published in B. H. Hill and C. K. Williams, *The Temple of Zeus at Nemea* (Princeton, 1966).
9 Pausanias 2. 15. 2.
10 Only preliminary reports of the excavations have been published. *Archaeological Reports* 1960/61, p. 5; 1961/2, p. 6.
11 Xenophon, *Hellenica* IV. iv. 5.
12 The original excavations are published in H. G. G. Payne *et al.*, *Perachora* (Oxford, 1940). Subsequent studies are J. J. Coulton, 'The Stoa by the Harbour at Perachora', *BSA* 1964, p. 100 f., and 'The West Court at Perachora', *BSA* 1967, p. 353 f.; H. Plommer and F. Salviat, 'The Altar of Hera Akraia at Perachora', *BSA* 1966, p. 207 f.; and R. A. Tomlinson, 'Perachora: the remains outside the sanctuaries', *BSA* 1969, p. 155 f.
13 The original excavators argue for a date in the ninth century, assuming the temple was built at the time that the first pottery was deposited in the sanctuary.
14 R. A. Tomlinson, *BSA* 1969, p. 193.
15 J. J. Coulton, *BSA* 1964, p. 100 f.
16 R. A. Tomlinson, *BSA* 1969, p. 172 f.
17 J. J. Coulton, *BSA* 1964, p. 100 f.
18 R. A. Tomlinson, *BSA* 1969, p. 157 f.
19 *Archaeological Reports* 1972/73, p. 8.
20 Plutarch, *Demetrios* 20.
21 This section depends on the excellent new analysis of this sanctuary by Birgitta Bergquist, *Herakles on Thasos*.
22 The principal evidence being the survival of a dialect otherwise spoken only in Cyprus, known to be a place to which Greeks migrated at the end of the Bronze Age.
23 C. Dugas, J. Berchmans and M. Clemmensen, *Le Sanctuaire d'Aléa Athéna à Tégée* (Paris, 1924).
24 P. Kavvadias, *Fouilles de Lycosoura* (Athens, 1893); V. Leonardos, *Excavations at Lycosoura* (in Greek); E. Levy, *Sondages à Lycosoura*, *BCH* 1967, p. 518 f.
25 *BCH* 1914.
26 G. Fougères, *Mantinée et l'Arcadie Orientale* (Paris, 1898), p. 103.
27 W. Reichel and A. Wilhelm, 'Artemis von Lusoi', *Jahreshefte* 1901, p. 1 f.
28 N. Yalouris, 'Excavations at Bassai', *Athens Annals* 1973, p. 55 (in Greek, with English summary).

8 EAST GREEK SANCTUARIES

1 Greek settlement in the Eastern Aegean and Asia Minor, J. M. Cook (Chapter XXXVIII of the revised *Cambridge Ancient History*, vol. II).
2 Excavation reports *Ath. Mitt.* 55 p. 1 f.; 58 p. 146 f.; 72 p. 52 f.; 74 p. 1 f. See also *Ath. Mitt.* 68 p. 1 f.; 72 p. 77 f.; 68 p. 25 f.
3 Thucydides I 13,3; I 15,3. See W. G. Forrest, *Colonisation and the rise of Delphi, Historia* 1957, 160 f.
4 Vitruvius VII praef. 11.
5 Pliny, *Natural History* XXXVI 90.
6 Herodotus II 148, in a sentence comparing its size with the temples at Ephesos and Samos.
7 The nineteenth-century excavations: J. T. Wood, *Discoveries at Ephesus* (1877), D. G. Hogarth, *Excavations at Ephesus,* 1908; the more recent work: Anton Bammer, *Die Architektur des Jüngeren Artemision von Ephesos* (Wiesbaden, 1972).
8 The story was narrated in the *Aithiopis* of Arktinos, the poem which followed the *Iliad* in the Epic Cycle.
9 The dimensions are not that different from those of the Samos temple.
10 For example, D. S. Robertson, *Handbook of Greek and Roman Architecture,* 2nd ed. (Cambridge, 1943), fig. 39.
11 Bammer.
12 Bammer, p. 9 f.
13 Bammer, p. 9 and p. 41 (fig. 43).
14 Th. Wiegand, *Didyma* (Berlin, 1941); G. Gruben, *JDI* 78 p. 78 f.; W. Hahland, *JDI* 79 p. 142 f.
15 Gruben, *JDI* 78 p. 87 f.
16 J. M. Cook and H. Plommer, *The Sanctuary of Hemithea at Kastabos* (Cambridge, 1966).
17 Strabo 14 634.
18 Labraunda: *Swedish Excavations and Researches,* Vol. 1 part 2, 'The Architecture of the Hieron' (Lund, 1963) (A. Westholm).
19 C. Humann, *Magnesia am Maeander* (Berlin, 1904).
20 Strabo 14. 1. 40; Vitruvius VII praef. 12.
21 Humann, p. 100 f.

Index

Bold type indicates main references

Abaton, 101
Acropolis, Athens, 17, 22, 37–40, 48, **78–90**, 105, 110, plates 22, 23, fig. 13
Adyton, 130
Aigina (town), 104
Alkibiades, 53
Alpheios, river, 56
Altars, 17, 37–9
  Aigina, Aphaia, 105–7, plate 38
  Argolid, Hera, 91–2
  Athens (Agora), twelve gods, 39
  Athens, Athena, 38, 80, 83–4, 88
  Delphi, Apollo, 66, plate 13
  Didyma, Apollo, 38, 136
  Ephesos, Artemis, 38, 126, 131–2, figs. 23, 24
  Epidauros, Asklepios, 97, 100
  Isthmia, Poseidon, 95
  Olympia, Zeus, 17, 27, 57
  Perachora, Hera, 39, 112–13
  Pergamon, Zeus, 17, 38–9, 132
  Samos, Hera, 125
  Syracuse, 39
  Thasos, Herakles, 116, 117
Altars, portable, 13
Altars, triglyph, 38–9, 95, 113
Altis, 57
Amasis, 125
Amazons, 128
Amphiktyones, 53, 56
Antigonos, 76, 115
Antiochos, 137
Apollonia, 51
Aratos, 109
Architects, 54, 83, 100, 109, 126, 129, 137
Argos (town), 90
Arignotos, 100
Asiatic bases, 133
Athens (town), 40
Attalos, 51, 69, 76, 137

Bacchiadai, 93
Baldacchino, 39
Bergquist, B., 106, 117
Berytus (Beirut), 76
Birmingham (City Museum), 130
Bouleuterion, 58–9
British Museum, 132
Bronze Age, Greek, 12, 20, 64, 71, 78, 80, 90, 108, 112, 117, 119, 122, 124, plate 23
Building stone, 36
Byzantium, 59

Caracalla, 24
Chaironeia, 109
Chalkotheke (armoury), 17, 18, 89
Chersiphron, 129
Christianity, 19, 24, 56, 71
Cnidos, 68
Corinthian order, 99, 100, 102, 108, 135
Corinthian pottery, 23, 93
Costs, 52–3
Crete, 11, 12, 13, 28, 39
Croesus, 36, 50, 56, 125, 128–9, 130–1
Crypt, 109
Cult statue, image, 16, 27–8, 62, 82, 86, 100, 110, 132–3
Cyrene, 59
Cyrus, 131

Darius, 22, 133
Dark ages, 15, 22, 90
Decoration, 35–7, 100
Delian alliance, 75
Demeter and Kore (Eleusis), 53
Demetrius, 76, 96, 115
Dialects, Greek, 11
Dining-rooms, 19, 42–4, 63, 87, 91, 95, 99, 101, 105, 111–14, 117–18, plates 5, 35, fig. 7
Dorian migration, 11
Doric order, 16, 34, 41, plate 2
Dörpfeld, W., 58

Earthquake damage, 25, 62
Ecbatana, 133, 135
Echo colonnade, 63
Egypt, Egyptian, 11, 32, 74, 76, 104, 125, 130, 132, 139
Eleusis, 53
Elis, 55, 59, 60
Ephesos (town), 128
Epidauros (town), 96
Erechtheus, 88
Etruscans, 32
Eumenes II, 39
Exedrai, 47, 99, plate 33
Expenditure, 52–3

Festivals, 41, 54
First fruits, 50
Fountain houses, 41, 45, 102, 106, 115, plate 6, fig. 8